D0038113

"You don't have to believe that Walsch is really speaking to God to find in this book a huge amount of wisdom and a perspective on reality worthy of serious consideration. There is something deeply inspired about this work. Neale Walsch has given us an important gift."

—*San Francisco Examiner & Chronicle* review of *Conversations with God, An Uncommon Dialogue, Books 1, 2,* and *3*

For Meg,

Conversations with God
for teens

Christmas
2004

Meg, I hope you enjoy
this book... I know you
know this stuff!
Be one of the
"Changers"

Love
Lisa
xo

NEALE DONALD WALSCH

Conversations with God
for teens

SCHOLASTIC INC.

New York   Toronto   London   Auckland   Sydney
Mexico City   New Delhi   Hong Kong   Buenos Aires

No part of this publication may be reproduced in whole or in part, or stored in a retrieval system, or transmitted in any form or by any means, electronic, mechanical, photocopying, recording, or otherwise, without written permission of the publisher. For information regarding permission, write to Hampton Roads Publishing Co., Inc., 1125 Stoney Ridge Road, Charlottesville, VA 22902.

ISBN 0-439-31389-9

12 11 10 9 8 7 6 5 4 3 2 1
2 3 4 5 6 7/0

Printed in the U.S.A.   01

First Scholastic printing, March 2002

Foreword

over the years i have, at times, been overwhelmed with how many emotions i've felt and how many questions i've found myself asking and the fiery passion by which these questions were fueled.

i've seen these questions cover the whole spectrum throughout my life . . . everything from "who is god and where do i go when i die?" . . . to "why am i here?" to "why do i feel so horrible about my body?" to "why is there such shame surrounding sex?" to "why war?". . . and millions of others in between (far too many to list!).

i felt many resistances brewing within me toward the answers i was being given in school and from those i was encouraged to look up to. there were many answers that heartened and resonated. there were also answers with the message being one of choicelessness, of patriarchy, of there being one singular goal in life toward which our whole lives were to be focused if we wanted to be successful (and answers about what "successful" itself meant).

there were messages of intolerance and judgment, of exclusion and competition. all of these messages (and many more) were at odds with what i felt somewhere within me. they seemed confusing and misleading, inconsistent, and hypocritical. and yet these views were at the center of what i was being taught. i was being sent the message of our being separate, of our being better or worse than each other, of there not being enough of *anything* to the point that we had to fight to get what we could, that i was *bad* if i wanted something that differed from what was perceived as *right* by my teachers or my community or society as a whole.

these and many other messages were absorbed by me . . . not without resistance, and not without confusion, but i tried them on for size in moments just the same. some i tried on for a millisecond and discarded; some i tried on for years, to be discarded later. some are still being mulled over today.

at that time i also chose not to revisit the religion i had left behind from the time i was 12 years old for what i perceived to be its hypocritical messages and its rigidity and exclusivity.

the most difficult part of my leaving it behind was the fact that i had been left with the challenge of establishing an entirely new relationship with god. with my religionlessness, i found myself not knowing where to begin. and while i believed in god, it would be years from the time i said goodbye to religion before i connected again with my newly defined god in a way that i felt clear and good about.

one day, after a tour that lasted a year and a half had ended, i sat alone in my backyard, a place i often sit in moments of deep reflection. an inner conflict had arisen out of my feeling both grateful beyond description for my being able to create and experience all that i had, *and* feeling uncomfortable with, overwhelmed, and disillusioned by how isolating and distancing (among many other things) these same experiences were.

i had achieved *everything* that i was taught by my family and the world at large to achieve. as i reflected i realized that these achievements felt like natural outcomes of my efforts and that my efforts were motivated by many different things.

of these motivations, there were two that i found to be the most obvious: the first one (and the biggest) being my desire to honestly express and understand myself and the world i lived in. the desire to then in turn *share* these personal revelations and love with people came from my feeling that it may validate others' experiences and offer encouragement or comfort if there was anything they could relate to.

i felt that it may have resulted in us feeling more connected if we found ourselves having had similar experiences. and that in my offering compassion to myself i might also be inspiring others to offer the same to *them*selves. and at the very least my expressions could be something that people had the opportunity to define themselves by in accordance to their loving or hating it.

the second motivating force was my desire to work well past the point of self-care to satisfy the curiosity i felt about what it was like to achieve the success that society was saying i *had* to achieve in order to be of any value as a person.

at this point in my life i had experienced what society had said was the *pinnacle* to attain yet i still felt like i was missing something. i was determined to understand what that was.

so i went to India with the intention of getting some distance from the pressure i felt to continue producing at breakneck speed. i went to reflect and to gain as much objectivity on my life as i could.

i joked with a friend that what i went to India to do i could have done in my own backyard, but it was easier to be in a place where i wouldn't hear "when's your next record coming out?" (a harmless enough question in and of itself, but not one that helped my situation at the time).

most importantly, i went *within* when i went to India. and while i was not completely unfamiliar with going within, i had never gone quite as deeply as this. what i found proved to be an even more awe-inspiring landscape than any country i'd ever been to.

i took this literal and figurative trip post first-dose-of-fame, post status-achieving, post manifesting my truest form of expression and experiencing all the results of that.

propelled by a desire to feel a kind of peace i had not yet experienced, i felt a great willingness to truly let go. of *everything*. i was willing to let go of every material possession i had, every symbol of status. i felt ready to do *anything* that i felt was needed to do to break through all the illusion and to find this peace. i was even willing to let go of any desire to express through writing and through music, which were forms of expression in which i had found such comfort from the time that i was very young.

all this is to say that i was ruthlessly ready to do what it took to be peaceful and i wasn't sure what that was.

a lot of what i had been doing was not working and i wasn't feeling the joy that i felt was my birthright (as it turns out, losing everything was *not* what was needed for me to find peace and clarity . . . but it *was* the *willingness* to do whatever it took and my *openness* to grow into very unfamiliar territories that i think played the biggest role in my eventually experiencing it).

i felt ready to let go of any expectations that i or anyone else had of me. wanting to see who my true friends were, i reevaluated every friendship. at one point i remember telling a friend that i wondered whether at this particular time it was time for me to die, because it felt like such a death of sorts (apparently not, and i'm glad about that). i investigated the voices in my head that played messages of anything other than love (and i am still editing these tapes to this day).

i wanted to get clear about what i felt my true purpose in life was: to evolve, express, define, accept, and love myself and to honor and encourage this in others as best as i can. i brought many of the things i had been taught into the light to see whether they helped serve this purpose. it was a beautiful and terrifying time. (i am now happy to feel that level of rebirth when i wake up in the mornings—not ALL the time—but a lot.)

my life didn't change as much, outwardly, as i was fully prepared for it to, but the shifts *inside* changed my relationship to many things.

there was a very life-altering book that i took with me on that trip to India that greatly impacted me and helped me cut through to my deepest truths in the way i did, and that book was *Conversations with God, Book 1*, by neale donald walsch. a friend of mine handed it to me shortly before i left on the trip. i think she saw the space i was in and felt this book might offer the encouragement and insight that i was ready to receive. it offered that and *so* much more.

in the finding of this book i immediately felt less alone . . . more understood. affirmed. i felt less *crazy*. many a recognition tear was shed during the reading of it. i felt validated and inspired and comforted. i felt connected with all of life and encouraged. i felt *recognized*. god in this book was how i had always envisioned god to be: unconditionally loving, consistent, and without expectation. it felt like *coming home*.

i know that this book came to me at the *perfect* time in my life. i *also* know that having the companionship of a book like this could have saved me from having many a moment of needless suffering and isolation in the years prior to my having read it.

i am so happy to know that this book is out there *now*, for you to read, if you choose, at this point in your life. and i am *very* happy to know that now there is a version of this message available for young people.

may you be touched by it the way i have been by this and all the *With God* books, and may you know that many people, of all generations, are proud and relieved to know that you are part of shaping the future.

i send a huge hug to you for the courage and openness it takes to read a book like this. and I thank you so much for your contribution here on this earth, regardless of what form it takes. whether it be considered grand or sweetly simple by your definition, i thank you.

and i believe the world thanks you. for being exactly who you are, right now.

take great care of yourself,
i send much love,

alanis morissette

Conversations with God
for teens

1

Finally, Answers

Suppose you could ask God any questions you wanted.

Questions like:

Why can't my parents stay in love and stay married?

Or . . .

How do you decide who gets to be Alanis Morissette or Michael Jordan, and who gets to live regular lives?

Or . . .

Why can't I just have sex and have it be okay with everybody? What's the big deal?

And suppose you received responses to your questions.

Responses like:

"Your parents *can* stay in love and stay married, but it would require a shift in the things they believe for them to do so. You can also be very okay and live a happy life if your parents do not stay together, but that would require a shift in the things *you* believe.

"I do not decide who gets to be Alanis Morissette and who gets to live regular lives. You do. You are making those choices right now. The problem is, you don't know that you're doing it— or how.

"You can have as much sex as you want, every day of your life, and it will be very okay with everybody. But first you must understand what sex is— and that may not be what you think."

Would you want to hear more?

You're about to.

This book contains questions just like that, from teenagers all over the world. The responses you'll find here have been placed here for your consideration only. This book has not come here to give you "the answers." The last thing you need is someone else giving you "the answers." The hope is that this book will place you in touch with your *own* answers.

When you are in touch with your own answers, the hopelessness that you may sometimes feel inside can be ended.

This book is the result of a conversation with God. Okay, okay, so you don't even know if there *is* a God, much less whether we can have a conversation, right? Don't worry about that right now. If you don't believe in God, consider this book a work of fiction. I won't mind. It'll still be a good read. Maybe the best book you've *ever* read.

I do think that God exists, and I do believe that God communicates with us. I have conversations with God all the time. How those conversations take place will be explained in just a few pages. For now, please consider the possibility that this book was brought into your life to change your life if you choose for it to, and to change the life of the world around you if that is also what you desire.

And don't think for a minute that it came to you by accident. *You called this book to you.*

You called this book to you because you live in an insane world, and you want to change it. Somewhere inside, somewhere deep inside, you know how life *could* be. You know that we are not supposed to be hurting each other here. You know that no one has the right to seek it all, to take it all, to hoard it all, while others have so little.

You know that might is not right. You know that truth is what matters, and openness and transparency and fairness, not hidden agendas and under-the-table dealings and behind-the-scenes maneuverings and getting the advantage. You know that when you get the advantage at the expense of someone else being *dis*advantaged, there is no advantage in that at all.

You know this, and you know more.

You know that so much of the stuff they teach in school is pointless. Where are the classes in Sharing Power, Cooperative Living, Accepting Differences and Celebrating Diversity, Shameless Sexuality, Understanding Unconditional Love?

Where are the courses in Sustainable Living, Responsible Economics, and Collective Consciousness? Where are the courses that are *relevant*? Cannot reading, writing, and arithmetic be taught *through* relevant courses, rather than *instead of them?*

Of course they can, and you know they can.

You know this, and you know more.

You know that our political systems on this planet suck. *They don't work.* We can't even elect a president and have every vote count. We can't even find a way to have the election *process* work, much less the process of politics *after* the election.

You know this, and you know more.

You know that hypocrisy reigns supreme in the lives of too many people. Not all people, but too many people. They say one thing and do another. And they think you don't see it; they think you're not watching, or that you're not smart enough to know that what you're looking at, pure and simple, is hypocrisy.

You know this, and you know more.

You know what is rewarded in this society and what is not, and that in this we have it all back ward. You know that we pay thirty million dollars for someone to play first base for the New York Yankees and thirty thousand dollars for someone to nurse our sick or teach our children or minister to our disheartened, and that this is crazy.

You know this, and you know more.

You know that you live in a society which keeps

trying to use the energy which *created* a problem to *solve* the problem; which uses killing to stop people from killing, which uses violence to put an end to violence, which uses injustice in the name of justice, inequality in the name of equality, intolerance in the name of tolerance, wars in the name of peace, and insanity in the search for a sane tomorrow.

What is wrong with this picture? you ask, and you *know* what is wrong. You don't need anyone to tell you. You only want someone to do something about it. You only want someone to be *able* to do something about it. Because until now, it's all looked pretty hopeless.

And why has it looked so hopeless? Basically, because everyone's lying about it. No one wants to tell it like it really is.

Well, all that's going to change.

Right here.

Right now.

With this book.

2

Truth Time

You tell the truth. That's what's cool about you.

I mean, you don't go around trying to kid yourself and trying to fool everybody else. You just *are*, and that's what it is, and if others don't like it, well, then that's what *that* is, and you're not going to change yourself because of something like that, right?

Okay, that means you're ready. Because people who *tell* the truth are usually ready to *hear* the truth. That's good, because we're going to do something really interesting here. We're going to have a conversation with God. But if you're not ready, it won't work.

Oh, the *conversation* part will work, because you can't stop that. All of us are having conversations with God, every minute of every day. What won't work is your ability to "get" it. You'll read it, but you won't get it. It's like a lot of things in life. You've got to be ready.

Right now most of the world is stuck. It's been stuck for half a century. Fifty-year-old ideas, half-century-old ways of doing things—that's what you see out there right now, *a lot*.

They're not ready. The people who live and breathe these ideas, I mean. The people who swear by them. They're not ready. Not for change, and not for the answers that would create change. Not most of them, anyway. Most of them aren't ready.

I think you are. So let me explain what's going on here.

I wrote a book called *Conversations with God* because I wanted to know why my life wasn't working, why it always seemed to have to be such a continuing struggle, what the rules were and how I could "play" and not lose all the time. I also wanted to know the point of it all.

What resulted from that call for help was a dialogue with God that I had in my mind and placed on paper. Other people found value in it and it wound up being translated into 27 languages.

My questions continued and more books followed. Then someone asked, "Why don't you do a book for teenagers?" And I said, "Because I wouldn't know what to ask about." And they replied, "Why not let *them tell you*?"

That's when I started asking teenagers, in person and through the Internet, *If you could ask God any question, what would it be?*

I received hundreds of replies. Here are some of them:

Why do You let children get abused sexually and physically? How come everyone wasn't born smart? Why is the world filled with hate?

What's the deal with the generation gap? Why can't parents just talk with us? And why is there so much pressure—from parents, from school, from everyone?

Is my life controlled by fate? Why are we taught facts, and not ideas, in school? Will I return to You, and will You be happy with me?

How come I have to pay adult ticket prices

at the movies when I'm 13, but I can't see an "R" movie? That's stupid. Why do we have to have three hours of homework after seven hours of school?

I'm confused and scared about what to make of my newly found sexual identity. How can I present that to the people I love?

How come people make such dumb laws? If You made us, then who made You?

How is that a God of mercy can be such an isolationist and so intolerant to other views? How can a God of infinite mercy condemn anyone for anything? Why condemn magic that heals? Why condemn for eternity those transgressions that are momentary?

Why is it that my parents notice only the things that I do wrong? How come adults want respect but don't give it back?

Why do people die? Why can't we live forever? What really is life after death?

Why is it that I can die for my country at 18, but I can't enjoy a cold beer on a hot day?

I feel as if I need to be successful—at everything. My parents seem to desperately want that. But what is "success"?

I don't know whether to hang with the popular "preppy" kids or the castoff "grungy" kids. Why does everyone have to separate?

Why do my parents freak out about sex? My God, they *freak* out.

Now aren't those great questions? They'll all be addressed here, as will many others that were asked—questions about dealing with authority, about choosing the right career, about drugs, about marrying or living together, about how the experiences of our lives are created, and even about what God looks like.

Let's get to one of those questions now, so you can see how the process plays out, and then I want to explain to you how my method of "receiving" the responses works.

This question was given to me by a young woman named Varinia.

 WHY DO YOU LET CHILDREN GET ABUSED SEXUALLY AND PHYSICALLY?

Varinia, my lovely, lovely friend, I know that you wish deeply in your soul that cruelty of all kinds could be eliminated from the Earth. So many people wish that, and so many are working for that.

11

There is so much sexual abuse in the world because there is so much sexual repression in the world. Humans have been taught from the time they were very young to be ashamed of their body parts and embarrassed or guilty about their sexuality. The result is that millions of people have sexual hang-ups you wouldn't believe.

Later in this conversation we'll talk about how you can help change all that, and how you can deal with whatever hang-ups the people around you may have. But you did not ask me why there was sexual and physical abuse in the world, you asked me why I *allowed* it—and I'm aware that that's an entirely different question.

YES, IT IS. SO WHY *DO* YOU ALLOW IT?

When I created life as you know it, I did so by simply separating myself into countless smaller parts of me. This is another way of saying that you were made "in the image and likeness of God."

Now because God is The Creator, that means that all of you are creators, too. You have free will, just as I have free will. If I had not given you free will, you could not create, but only react. If you could only do what I tell you to do, then you could not create, but only obey.

Obedience is not creation. It is an act of sub-servience, not an act of power. God is not sub-servient to anyone, and since you are a part of God, you are, by nature, not subservient to any-one, either.

That is why, when you are *made* to be sub-servient, you immediately revolt. It is against your very nature. It is a violation of Who You Are at the very core of your being.

Teenagers know this more than anyone.

BUT WHAT ABOUT THOSE HUMAN BEINGS WHO HAVE DONE THINGS WITH THEIR FREE WILL THAT HAVE BEEN VERY HURTFUL TO OTHERS?

There have been many people like that, and it is true that I could have stopped this. I did not stop it because the Process of Life itself is the expression of free will. Anything less than that is not life, but death.

Even when the expression of free will does not serve the highest good, it must be allowed, or freedom itself is a mockery.

The word "freedom" and the word "God" are interchangeable. You cannot have one with-out the other. For God to exist, freedom must exist.

The beauty of freedom, however, is that it

can be expressed by all beings, not just a few. This means that the people of the Earth are free to *eliminate* the experiences of sexual abuse and physical abuse from their collective experience forever.

They are also free to eliminate other conditions of cruelty and misery that they now endure.

HOW?

That is the question this book will answer.

Now that's the kind of dialogue you're going to find throughout the rest of this book. All of the "lead" questions—the questions that start off a portion of the dialogue—came from young people just like yourself. Some of the follow-up questions are questions that I asked, because I felt that those asking the *first* question would have asked the follow-ups if they had the chance.

To understand more fully how this "conversation" process works, it will help you to know that, as I've said, all of us are having conversations with

God every day—and that includes you. You just may not have called them that.

God is talking to all of us, all the time. We are continually being communicated with by the universe. Life is constantly telling Life about Life. Life is always sending us messages.

True wisdom may be found in the chance utterance of a friend you meet on the street; in the lyrics to the next song you hear on the radio; the words that confront you, big as life, on the billboard around the next corner; the voice that you hear whispering inside your head—or this book . . . that "just happened" to come into your hands.

Now substitute the word "God" for the words "true wisdom" in the above sentence and you will understand how your conversation with God works. God has never, *ever* stopped inspiring the human race—and God inspires us by sending us *messages*—ideas, thoughts, song lyrics, words for a book . . . you name it.

In my own life, God's conversations most often take the form of thoughts that fill my head, especially when I am asking for help with a serious question—

15

and when I am willing to be quiet enough to hear the answer. God "speaks" to me in a voice that doesn't sound like anyone's voice in particular. It is what I have called a "voiceless voice," something like the voice of your own thoughts.

Now you might say, "Well, they *are* your own thoughts! What makes you think this is the voice of God?" That's a fair question. When I asked God that question, here's the answer that I heard:

> Neale, if I was going to communicate with you, how else would I do it? Wouldn't "putting thoughts into your head" be one of the most effective ways?
>
> When Thomas Aquinas had "thoughts in his head" about theology, wasn't he said to have been "inspired by God"?
>
> When Amadeus Mozart had "thoughts in his head" about music, wasn't he said to have been "inspired by God"?
>
> When Thomas Jefferson had "thoughts in his head" about freedom, wasn't he said to have been "inspired by God" to write a declaration about "one nation, under God"?
>
> How do you think that I communicate with people if it is not by putting "thoughts in their head"? Do you think that I show up at their doorstep in a long white robe and hand them a

scroll? Do you think that I appear in a cloud of mist over their bed and boom my wisdoms into the air? Would that be more believable to you?

Is this how you have it? That the more unbe-lievable something is, the more believable it is?

I'll tell you this: I come to people *in the way that is most believable.* I do this for a very good reason. *I want to be believed.* Yet even then you do not believe me.

For most people, the most believable way for God to show up in their lives would be as an apparition, with me appearing in robes and handing over a tablet. I have done those things, yes. *But do you think I am limited to those things?*

More often—much more often—I come to people in a much more natural way, as a much more integral part of life itself. This could be as a thought, as a feeling, or as an inspiration, just as I'm coming to you now through the feelings you are having and the words you are hearing and the paragraph that is coming to you in this way.

Those are the words that came, and that's how the process works.

Now it might sound good if I said that I ponder

my questions for hours, meditating and praying and remaining in the stillness until I am brought to enlightenment and tremble with the energy of God flowing through my fingertips. But the truth is, I put down the first thing that comes to my head. There's no editing, no changing, no "toning down" or "fixing up." It's just a matter of "hearing" it and writing it down. It's just like taking dictation.

I've been doing this for ten years now, ever since the circumstances of my life caused me to reach out to God and beg for help. This latest book was written just for you, just for teenagers, not only because someone suggested it, but also because I've received hundreds of letters from teenagers all over the world telling me how impacted they were by the original *Conversations with God* books—and loaded with additional questions!

Some of the teenagers who asked these questions said that I could use their full identity, and others asked me not to. So what I've done, just to keep everything uniform, is use first names and ages only, and locations when they said it was all right, and even the word "anonymous" when they said they wanted it that way.

After two years of talking to young people like yourself and collecting questions, I asked a young person just like you to be my assistant and to put them all into categories so that I could approach them in some kind of sequence.

In a few cases I sent the response back to the teenagers asking the question, to see if it brought up any reaction or further question from them. As I said, I've also added some questions of my own that I thought the original questioners would have asked if they could have been here to keep the conversation going. They are also questions that *I* wanted to ask, on my own. I put those in here, too. And so I mingled my voice with yours, and in this way I created a dialogue.

Sometimes the responses I received were directed right to me, and sometimes they were directed to the person asking the original question. *I believe that some might also be directed right to you, reading this book.*

It was very exciting for me to create this book, and I feel, in your reading it, there is a possible magic about to happen.

The first thing that will occur as you see the questions and read the responses is that you will (a) agree with a response, (b) disagree with a response, (c) fall somewhere in between. Then will come the magic. This will be the moment when the responses cause you to notice what *you* think and how *you* feel. You'll be placed in touch with your own wisdom within. That's the wonder and the magic of every good conversation, and it is the purpose of all of your conversations with God.

3

The Changers

You guys are fascinating and want to know everything. You haven't stopped asking questions yet. Some adults are like that, but many are not. Too many. They've bought into a religion, or a philosophy, or a political party, or all three, and they're done asking questions. They think they've got the answers.

They don't. The world today is not acting as if it has any answers at all that make sense. But most of

the world is not ready to hear this. I think that you
are. That doesn't make you better. It just makes you
different. Different is not better; it's just different.

It's important for you to know the difference.

It is also important for you to know the difference that *you* can make because you *are* different.

Look, you guys are at the edge of it. You're at
the furthermost point. But you have to know, I
have to tell you, that being different just for the
sake of being different is child's play. Being different for the sake of *making* a difference is another
thing altogether. That's for those who want their
lives to count for something. Not in the eyes of
others (you already know that isn't important), but
in their own eyes.

There are some people who make a real difference on this planet with their lives, and these people can ultimately change the world.

They may not change it by becoming world
leaders and impacting the entire planet (although
some of them certainly will); they may not change
it by standing above the crowd and saying "follow
me" (although some of them will); and they may
not change it by writing best-selling books or
appearing in meaningful movies or singing signifi-
cant songs (although some of them will).

They will change it by quietly moving through

the world, largely unseen but always remembered by those whose lives they touch. They will change it by being different. By acting in a different way. By marching to a different drummer. By living *life* differently—as if they had different rules.

This is what is meant by being different not simply to be different, but to *make a difference*.

Now some might say, *What difference does it make? Nothing ever changes!* Ah, but those who say this do not know that our individual lives *can* change, and the world can change, too. There are people—many of them teenagers—who are lifting the collective consciousness around them right now. Some are doing it in very public ways, some in private ways, but they are doing it.

These are The Changers. It's just the way they are. It's just *who* they are. Everything changes the moment they walk into a room. Everything gets lighter, feels different. Suddenly, it's all good. And the world, if only for that moment, becomes a nicer place.

You know the kind of person we're talking about. You can be that kind of person. You may be showing up like that right now. You may already be one of The Changers. The question is not whether you are a Changer, but what it is that you next seek to change.

All of this is what led you to this book. As I told you, you called it to you. It may have come to you by an indirect route, but that doesn't mean you didn't make an active choice to read it. At some level you did, believe me, or you wouldn't be holding it in your hands. You may have called the book to you at a subconscious level, but *you called it to you.*

Why? Because you want changes, and you want them now. Not next year, not some other time, not some day "in the future," but right now. Because you're ready.

You are ready to experience, right here, right now, the wisdom that resides within you, the courage that is yours, and the truth in your heart. You are anxious to apply that truth to life. You'd like the whole world to apply its highest truths, because there *must be another way to live.* You know that. That's obvious to you.

Like I said, a lot of people don't want to find new answers, or create changes. Not now. Not ever. They're not willing to look at the way things are, much less at the way they could be.

They're not ready.

You are. You *definitely* are if you've read *this* far.

4

The Dialogue Begins

As I began putting this manuscript together, I knew that I wanted to tell you of other resources that I knew about that deal with the questions and the issues many younger people are confronting. So, you will notice that throughout these pages, every so often, you will see a small numeral, like the one right here,[1] inserted into the text. This is what is known as an "endnote" reference.

At the very end of the book you'll find short

notes carrying the corresponding numeral and re-
lating directly to what has just been read. Usually it
will be some additional material or resource that I
wish to recommend to you. You can flip back there
to see what each note is all about when these
appear, without the note itself interrupting the
flow of the book.

Now, as I pondered where to begin this dialogue, I thought of those questions that I heard
over and over again, in one form or another, everywhere I went. These are the questions that were
begging to be answered. So I started there, punch-
ing them into the computer and following with the
first thing that came to my head. I trust that God
inspired the response—and all the responses to all
the questions in this book.

Let the dialogue begin . . .

**WHY IS THE WORLD THE WAY IT IS? WHY CAN'T WE
STOP THE KILLING AND THE SUFFERING? WHY CAN'T
WE FIND A WAY TO GET ALONG, TO BE NICE TO EACH
OTHER, TO LOVE EACH OTHER? AND IS IT ALWAYS
GOING TO HAVE TO BE THIS WAY? IS THERE NOTH-
ING THAT ANYONE CAN DO TO CHANGE IT? SHOULD
I JUST GIVE UP, HAVE NO HOPE, FORGET TRYING TO
MAKE THINGS DIFFERENT, BECAUSE IT'S NOT GOING
TO WORK ANYWAY?**

OKAY, GOD—IF THERE *IS* A GOD—WHAT'S UP?

Am I glad you asked *that*. Good question. A *bunch* of good questions. And a very good place to start.

But first, thanks for coming to this dialogue. Thanks for giving me a chance to talk with you this way. I'm talking with you all the time (which is something that you may or may not realize), but not in this way. So I'm glad to have this direct line of communication open between us.

Oh, and by the way, yes, I do exist. There is a God.

We'll talk more about that later, too. Right now I don't want to get off the topic here. These first questions are very important.

The world is the way it is because that is the way human beings have created it. It is not necessary for the world to be this way, but it is necessary for life to reflect your every thought about it. The collective thoughts of the human race, and its aggregate ideas from the beginning of time until now, are reflected in the world in which you live.

Your species has not been able to stop the killing and the suffering because your species has had a Killing and Suffering mentality.

Those who have come before you have

believed that killing is justified as a means of resolving their disagreements or getting what they want, or think they need.

They have also believed that suffering is a normal part of life. Some of them have even said that it is *required by God*.

It is from these beliefs that the present human experience has arisen. It is out of these understandings that your elders create their everyday reality—and yours.

You *can* find a way to get along, to be nice to each other, and to love each other, but it would require you to give up these beliefs, and that is not something that those who have come before you have been willing to do.

Do not give up hope, do not ever stop trying to change the world, unless you are satisfied with the world the way it is. There is only one reason to change the world—or to change any-thing—and that is in order to make a statement of Who You Are.

This is the purpose of all of life.

? **WHAT IS THE PURPOSE OF LIFE? I DON'T UNDERSTAND THIS. WHAT ARE YOU SAYING HERE? WHAT IS THE POINT OF LIFE, AND OF IT BEING THE WAY IT IS? WHAT IS THE MEANING OF LIFE?**
—Adria, 18

The point of Life is to provide a way in which All That Is (which many of you call "God") can know Itself experientially.

Put another way, Life is God, experiencing Itself.

IF LIFE THE WAY WE'RE LIVING IT ON THIS PLANET—WITH ALL THE KILLING, ALL THE SUFFERING, ALL THE GREED AND SELFISHNESS—IS "GOD EXPERIENCING ITSELF," THEN I DON'T WANT TO HAVE ANYTHING TO DO WITH GOD.

That's understandable, because right now, you don't see The Gift.

WHAT GIFT?

The Gift that I have given to the human race.

YOU CALL THE WAY LIFE IS NOW A "GIFT"?

Yes, because you are getting it exactly the way you want it. You are always having your way.

29

THAT'S NOT THE WAY MOST TEENAGERS EXPERI-ENCE IT. IN FACT, I DON'T KNOW ANY TEENAGERS WHO EXPERIENCE IT THAT WAY.

Life is not the way most teenagers want it because teenagers are not the most power-ful people in your world, and your world is presently being created by the most powerful people among you. For the most part, those are members of the older generation. And not all of them, only a tiny percentage of them.

I KNOW, I KNOW. THAT'S THE PROBLEM!

When you decide as a species that it is no longer going to be this way, it will no longer be that way.

YEAH, RIGHT. TEENAGERS ARE GOING TO TAKE OVER THE WORLD.

Teenagers are not going to take over the world. And, in truth, you wouldn't want them to. It takes the combined wisdom of all ages to make the kind of world in which you wish to live—a well-rounded world with differing points of view, filled with people of differing experiences, offering everyone the fun and the excitement of creating jointly acceptable outcomes from differing starting places.

So no, teenagers are not going to take over the world. But in years to come all people will have more to say about their lives and their future, if you decide that this is the way you want it.

SURE.

Really. The reason that a tiny percentage of the people control the lives of the largest number is because the larger number allows it to.

HOW CAN THEY STOP IT FROM HAPPENING, WHEN THE SMALLER NUMBER OF PEOPLE HAVE ALL THE POWER? YOU JUST SAID SO YOURSELF. THEY HAVE THE POWER.

Power is something that is given. It cannot be taken. It is given. And it is given away because those who give it away think that they are powerless. The irony is that they are powerless because they have given their power away. In truth, they have all the power they want. They simply don't want it.

31

YEAH, TEENAGERS HAVE ALL THE POWER THEY WANT, THEY JUST DON'T WANT IT. RIGHT.

It's true. Think about it for a moment. The power that your parents have over you is power that you give them. If you did not want to give them power, they would have none. If you did not want to do what they told you to do, there is nothing they could do about it.

The reason that teenagers give their power to their parents is that their parents have something that teenagers want. This could be anything from love to a place to live, food and clothes to money with which to buy what you want, a car for you to drive, or whatever.

As soon as you no longer want what your parents have, or no longer need it, your parents have lost complete control of you. In the meantime, you are simply using your behavior (in this case, your obedience to your parents) as a means of getting what you want. This is one exercise of power.

IT SOUNDS LIKE MANIPULATION TO ME.

It is, if it is done dishonestly. It is not, if it is done openly, honestly, with everyone understanding your agenda, and you understanding everyone else's. Then you have a shared agenda, mutual goals, and there is nothing manipulative in that.

So, it turns out, it is you who are the powerful one.

I NEVER THOUGHT OF IT THAT WAY.

That is why you have brought yourself to this book. Because you are ready to. The conversation we will have here will bring you many insights, and reveal many secrets.

SO YOU ARE SAYING THAT THE OPPRESSED PEOPLE OF THE WORLD ARE NOT REALLY OPPRESSED? THEY ARE "POWERFUL"?

I am saying that at some point in time there was something that they wanted, and they traded in their power for that.

Maybe they thought that those who are now oppressing them would give them security, or a better life, so the largest number of those "oppressed" people looked the other way. Maybe they thought that if they did *not* look the

other way, but, rather, complained and began to
revolt, that they would be killed. Since what
they "wanted" was to live, no matter *what* the
circumstances, they *got what they wanted.*

That is true power. True power is getting
what you want.

**OH, SURE, WHEN THE ALTERNATIVE IS DEATH, YOU'RE
GETTING WHAT YOU "WANT" BY NOT COMPLAIN-
ING. YEAH, RIGHT. BOY, YOU'VE GOT A PRETTY
WEIRD WAY OF SEEING THINGS.**

Wait a minute! There *are* those who have
chosen the alternative. Brave people in all nations
and times have made that choice. That is why
humans have always honored those who have
struggled, and died, to make others free.

The people who worked hard in the beginning to create the United States and to free
themselves from what they felt was the tyranny
of Great Britain did so at the risk of losing
everything, no?

The signers of the Declaration of Indepen-
dence said that, in the cause of freedom, they
were pledging their "lives, their fortunes, and
their sacred honor." And they were.

The founding fathers of America said things

like, "Give me liberty or give me death." *And they meant it.*

Against such courage, oppressors have no power. In moments of such declarations it becomes clear where the true power really lies—and *where it has always been.*

This has been demonstrated throughout human history. As soon as those who were oppressed decided that they were *not* living a better life, but rather a life not worth living, they took their power back, and dismantled their government. The very government that was supposed to be so powerful suddenly fell, silent and weak, unable to do anything about its own dismantling.

This is exactly what happened not only in those old British Colonies now known as the United States, but all over the world. Some more recent examples include the former Soviet Union, the former Yugoslavia, and South Africa, to name just a few.

Where the people have said, "This far, and no further," the oppression stops. Where the people have still not gathered the will or the strength to do that, the oppression continues.

It is the same in your own household. It is the same in your own life.

As soon as you decide that you would rather not have what you have been trading your power for, you reclaim that power and then get what you choose.

What you have reclaimed is the inherent power with which you have been born. This is called Original Power. It is the essence of Who You Really Are.

This is what I have termed The Gift.

"ORIGINAL POWER," HUH?

Yes.

WE ALL HAVE IT?

Yes.

EVEN BABIES?

Yes, only they don't know it. They don't remember. Most people don't remember, even when they get older. Most adults still do not remember. They are living in what could be described as a state of amnesia, in which they have forgotten that they have this Original Power.

WHAT IS THIS POWER, AND WHAT CAN WE DO WITH IT?

It is the Power of God. It is MY power. It is Who and What I Am. Have you not been told that you have been made "in the image and likeness of God"?

I'VE HEARD THAT, YEAH.

Yet most of you do not know what this means. You think that you have been born in Original Sin, and you believe this. I tell you now that you have been born in Original Power.

WHAT CAN WE DO WITH IT? YOU DIDN'T ANSWER MY QUESTION BEFORE. WHAT CAN WE DO WITH IT?

Create.

CREATE?

Create. Original Power is the power to create.

CREATE WHAT?

Anything you like. Whatever you choose.

37

YEAH, RIGHT.

Really. This power is not just what you have, it is what you ARE. You have, and are, the power to create. And if you knew this, your whole life would change.

5

The Way the
World Is

**IF WE'RE ALL SUPPOSED TO HAVE THIS ORIGINAL
POWER, HOW DOES IT WORK, AND WHY DON'T
MORE PEOPLE USE IT?**

Let's go to the second question first. Most
people don't use it because they do not know

they have it. They believe themselves to be powerless in the face of Life, and what they believe, they experience.

The second half of that answer is the answer to the first half of your question.

"What they believe, they experience"—*that is how the power works.*

WE GET TO EXPERIENCE WHATEVER WE BELIEVE WE WILL EXPERIENCE?

That's right.

I DON'T BELIEVE THAT.

And so, of course, you won't experience it. And this is true of most of the world. Nearly all the people in the world deny their own power. They do not believe that they have it. And that is why the world is the way it is.

SPEAKING OF WHICH, THERE ARE A LOT OF QUESTIONS ABOUT THE WORLD AND HOW IT IS THAT WE WANT TO ASK. CAN WE BEGIN WITH THOSE?

Absolutely.

OKAY, HERE GOES. DO THESE HAVE TO BE IN ANY ORDER?

No.

 HOW COME EVERYONE WASN'T BORN SMART?
—Danny

Danny, I want to tell you a great secret. Everyone IS born "smart." Everyone comes to their physical life knowing everything they need to know to do exactly what they came here to do. But not everyone came here to do the same thing.

Some souls came to their body to do one thing, and some to do another. So some seem to be "brighter" or "smarter" in certain academic subjects in school, and others seem to do better in other subjects, or have different gifts altogether.

Everybody comes with the right and perfect gift to give to be themselves. And so, you have nothing to learn. You have only to remember what you have always known.

No one has to teach a baby how to trust. No one has to teach a child how to love. To the newborn of your species, these things come naturally. *They bring this understanding with them.*

Life is not a process of discovery. It is a process of creation. You are not *learning* Who You Are, you are *recreating* Who You Are, by remembering all that you have always known, and choosing what you now wish to experience of your Self.

 WHY IS THE WORLD FILLED WITH HATE?
—*Danny, 19, Miami*

People hate each other because they have the wrong idea about each other. They also have the wrong idea about life and how it is.

These ideas have become "beliefs," and that has made them very powerful. You see, Danny, what you believe, you experience.

WHY?

Because that is how the power that I have given you works. It is the power to create. It is Original Power, the power you were born with, the power that is YOU.

This power to create works in you in three ways:

42

In your thoughts

In your words

In your actions

AND "BELIEFS" ARE THOUGHTS?

That's right, and so they have the power of creation behind them. What you think, what you say, and what you do, you become.

And that is why the world is the way it is.

YOU THINK WE BELIEVE THAT THE WORLD SHOULD BE THE WAY IT IS? NO WAY. NOBODY THAT I KNOW BELIEVES THE WORLD SHOULD BE THE WAY IT IS.

It is the larger belief *system* of the humans who are in charge of your planet that is the problem, not the individual beliefs of you and your friends.

WHAT DO YOU MEAN?

As I said, the people of Earth live out a life that is based on how most people believe life is. Life does not have to be this way, but they believe that it does. The belief system of the human race is based on a whole series

43

of understandings which are, in fact, *mis*understandings.

When these beliefs change, the world will change.

? **WHY DO SO MANY PEOPLE HAVE NOTHING, NO FOOD, CLOTHES, OR HOME? WHY DO YOU PUT PEOPLE IN THAT POSITION?** —*Zoar*

This is a perfect example of just what I'm saying here. I do not put people in that position, Zoar. Human beings do. They do because they believe that there is "not enough."

People believe that there is not enough money, not enough food, not enough clothing or shelter to go around. They believe, in fact, that there is not enough of *any* of the "stuff of life" to allow everyone to survive and be happy.

Because people believe this, they think that they have to *compete with each other* in order to get "the stuff of which there is not enough."

The illusion of insufficiency is a major illusion of humans. So many of the decisions and actions of your species are based on this illusion.

If you really think there is "not enough" of something that you really need to survive (much less simply be happy), you will fight tooth and nail to get as much of it as you can. The human race has done this for thousands of years.

You will turn everything into competitions. Your economics will be competitions, the winners of which get the most money. Your politics will be competitions, the winners of which get the most power. Your religions will be competitions, the winners of which get the most heavenly reward.

Some members of the human species even think that there is "not enough" heaven to go around, so they are competing with each other to get in!

All of this is insane, given that there is enough of everything for everyone. But most members of the human race don't know this, and so they compete ruthlessly. They even kill each other for *the stuff of which there is not enough*.

All that is required, Zoar, for every person to have sufficient food, clothing, and shelter is for the people of the Earth to share and share alike. If they did, they would find that there is more than enough for everyone to live happily.

You can help the world understand this. By stepping outside of the illusion, by rejecting the idea of insufficiency, you can demonstrate to everyone around you What Is True About That.

Just share. And share grandly. Give more than you think you have to give, and you will discover that "there's more where that came from."

? **WHAT'S IT LIKE TO SEE YOUR CHILDREN SIT AROUND AND DESTROY (OR TAKE FOR GRANTED) EVERYTHING YOU HAVE GIVEN US?**
—Ariel

If I had an investment in outcomes, you would think it would be depressing, but I have no investment in the outcome of the adventure we are taking together. There is no one way that I "need" things to "be."

If there was a way that I really wanted things, do you suppose that I could not have them that way? What kind of a God would I be if I couldn't?

I did not create life to "get my way." I created life to let you get yours. By this process I DO get my way, because what I choose is for you to decide who and what you are, and who and what you wish to be—both as individuals and as a society.

What I observe is that many humans "sit around and destroy" (or take for granted) much of what they have, and that this does not serve them. It does not allow them to experience what they say they wish to experience.

They are saying that they want to go to Seattle, but they are heading for San Jose. They are saying that they want a world of peace, harmony, and love, and that they wish their lives to be filled with joy, happiness, and abundance, but they are doing everything that works against peace, harmony, and love, and making it virtually impossible to experience joy, happiness, and abundance.

Interestingly, this is not because they do not know how. Humans have been given all the tools with which to create the life of their highest dreams. They simply choose not to use them.

WHY?

Because they do not believe that these tools work, or because they do not even remember that they have them, or because, as we've already discussed, they are invested in keeping things more or less the way they are.

47

I STILL DON'T GET THAT. WHO WOULD WANT TO KEEP THINGS THE WAY THEY ARE?

Anyone who believes that the way life is being lived right now on your planet is the way it has to be lived in order to survive. Anyone whose basic beliefs about life are supported by those misunderstandings I was referring to earlier.

CAN YOU GIVE ME ANOTHER EXAMPLE?

Well, in addition to the illusion of insufficiency that we just talked about, there is the illusion of disunity.

Most humans believe that they are separate from each other, that they are not part of one body. They believe that they are separate from their environment, that they are not part of one system. And they believe that they are separate from God, that they are not part of One Being.

This belief in disunity is killing them—and you.

 SPEAKING OF THAT, WHEN WILL THE WORLD COME TO AN END?—*Leonte, Miami, Florida*

The problem is not the world coming to an end. The problem is the world becoming uninhabitable by the human species. That, Leonte, is a different matter altogether.

If things continue the way they are going, the world "as you know it" could cease to exist within your lifetime. The Earth itself will go on.

There is no reason for it not to exist for millions of years. It has already existed that long and it has the capability of doubling its present life span easily.

So, the question is not, how long will the Earth exist? The question is, how long will it be inhabitable by a species of beings such as yours? That is the question, and only you have the answer.

This is something you must now decide. Indeed, you are deciding it every day, through your actions.

Many of you are pretending that you do not know this, or that you will ultimately outsmart the process of degradation and devolution that your actions have begun.

These are illusions, and you may wish to explore whether it would be to your benefit to step outside of them and create a new cultural story.

 WHY DOES THE WORLD HAVE ITS PRIORITIES SO MIXED UP? ARE TEENAGERS THE ONLY

ONES WHO KNOW WHAT'S REALLY IMPORTANT, AND THAT IT'S NOT "MAKING MONEY," OR "GET-TING TO THE TOP," OR "BEING FAMOUS" OR ANY OF THOSE THINGS?

—Neil, 16, West Allis, Wisconsin

Sometimes it does seem as though young people are far more in touch with what's truly important in life, given how the human race itself says it wishes to experience life.

Older adults often say one thing and do another. They say they want to live long and healthy and happy lives, for instance, and then they smoke and drink and put themselves under incredible stress striving to acquire and accumulate things that, to younger people, have no meaning.

This pushing and straining to "get ahead" or even to just "stay afloat" is behavior based in fear—something which younger people do not have much of. The fear is, of course, that there is "not enough," as I pointed out earlier.

This fear is lived so completely that it actually becomes part of the human experience at many times and in many places. In other words, it's not just a "thought" that people have, it has become their on-the-ground reality.

This "reality" then reconfirms the original

thought, and a vicious circle has been created. Thought precedes reality, and creates it. Reality confirms thought, and reinforces it. Thought creates further reality, creating further thought, creating further reality, and pretty soon the whole place is spinning in its illusions, living in an Alice in Wonderland world where everyone will swear that what is real is NOT real, and that what is NOT real is real.

It is not *real* that "fame and fortune" are the source of all happiness in life, and older adults say they know this—then they go ahead and behave as if it were real anyway. They say one thing, and do another.

You younger adults are having none of it. You know the truth, you have no need for money and material success, no yearning to "climb the corporate ladder."

MY FATHER WOULD SAY, "YES, WELL, JUST WAIT A FEW YEARS. IT'S EASY TO TALK THAT WAY NOW, BUT WAIT UNTIL YOU'VE GOT TO SUPPORT YOURSELF, MUCH LESS A WIFE AND FAMILY. HOW DO YOU THINK I'VE PUT A ROOF OVER YOUR HEAD, AND THOSE CLOTHES ON YOUR BODY? IT'S TIME TO WAKE UP, SON."

There is such a thing as being responsible for yourself. This is what your father is talking about. He only wants you to be happy in life. He only wants you to be able to take care of yourself, and those you love. So, his motives are genuine and real, and based in love.

Yet there is more than one way to get to happiness, and more than one way to take care of yourself, and more than one way to provide for those you love.

The world right now is approaching these challenges in the way it always has for thousands of years. It is basing its approach on the data currently on hand about life and how it is. What could prove beneficial here is new data.

New data about reality, and what is *really* "real." New data about life, and how your reality is really created. New data about you, and who you really are.

That's what this conversation is about, because young people today are under more pressure than ever before to "perform" in some particular way in the world, and they are trying to do that while working with two sets of data— the data that the world of older people is giving them, and the data that exists in their hearts.

THAT'S RIGHT! THAT'S EXACTLY RIGHT! YOU'VE HIT IT RIGHT ON THE HEAD.

6

The Pressure of Being a Teenager

 WHY IS THERE SO MUCH PRESSURE—FROM PARENTS, FROM SCHOOL, FROM EVERYONE?

—15-year-old boy in Oregon

Pressure is a condition of life, but there is probably more of it felt during your teenage years than almost any other time of your life.

There will always be someone who wants something from you. If they want it from you more than you want to give it, or faster than you can do it, you feel the pressure.

Even if all they want is what *you* want, you can feel pressure to keep your word and do what you said you were going to do.

So pressure is a part of teen life, for sure. But it can be a good part. It needn't bother you. It can be present, but it needn't be a negative. It can be a positive.

The pressure in your tires is what keeps them rolling. The pressure in a cooker is what produces the meal.

Thus, pressure can be good. If you keep the pressure on, you can accomplish things. Sometimes, even great things. This is called "creative stress."

The whole universe, in fact, is a stress system. One thing is pulling against the other all the time. This is what creates balance. It's actually what keeps everything in place.

I DON'T FEEL LIKE EVERYTHING'S IN PLACE. I FEEL LIKE I'M UNDER TOO *MUCH* PRESSURE.

Pressure is a delicate thing. Too much of it pulls things *out* of place. Everything gets out of balance.

This is the kind of pressure you're talking about. It can come from parents, and it can show up a lot at school.

Much of this pressure comes from the conflicting sets of data with which young people are working. Their heart is telling them one thing about life, the outside world is telling them something else.

AS I SAID, THAT'S RIGHT. SO HOW DO I DEAL WITH IT? HOW CAN I GET MY PARENTS AND MY SCHOOL TO GET WITH IT?

It would be inaccurate to assume that your point of view about things is what is "right," and that the view of your parents and the school is what is "wrong."

Later on we'll talk about this concept of "right" and "wrong," and how those two polarities don't really exist. For now, it might be helpful to consider the possibility that what works in the life that you are collectively creating in your world may lie somewhere in between. In other words, you are not entirely "right," and older adults are not entirely "right," either.

Explain to your parents what your priorities are, and the important things in life that you have identified, upon which you base these priorities. Then ask them to explain to you theirs (even though you've heard it before a million times). See if there is anyplace where the two can meet.

AND IF THERE ISN'T?

Then you may start to believe that you are getting "pressure" from your parents, and that may not be what is actually happening. It may seem as if you and your parents have entirely different interests. This is not what I have observed to be true, but I can see that it certainly looks true to you, from where you are seeing things. So it will seem as though a lot of pressure is coming at you from your parents and from school.

OH, BELIEVE ME, THERE'S PRESSURE FROM EVERY-WHERE. A LOT OF IT COMES FROM MY OWN FRIENDS, TOO. SOMETIMES THEY WANT ME TO DO SOME-THING, OR ACT IN A WAY, THAT DOESN'T FEEL LIKE "ME." I'M NEVER SURE WHAT TO DO. IF I STAY TRUE TO MYSELF, I'M ON THE OUTS WITH THE

**GROUP. IF I STAY TRUE TO THE GROUP, I'M NOT
BEING MYSELF.**

Remember this for the rest of your life. It
may be one of the most important things you
will ever hear:

*Betrayal of yourself in order not to betray
another is betrayal nonetheless. It is the highest
betrayal.*

If you are trying to avoid betraying another
but must betray yourself in the process, then
you are still committing betrayal. It is merely
a question of *whom* you are betraying, not
whether you are betraying.

Yet when you are betraying yourself, you are
betraying another as well, because the "you"
that they think you are is not who you are at all.
It is a false you. You have betrayed yourself *and*
another.

Therefore never betray yourself. Remember
the words of Polonius to Hamlet, written by
William Shakespeare:

"To thine own self be true, and it must follow as the night the day, thou canst not then be
false to any man."

Do not worry about "the group." The group
will go away. One day it will simply not be there.

Yet *you* will *never* go away. You will be with your Self until the end of time.

DOES THAT MEAN TO ONLY DO WHAT I WANT TO DO?

It means, decide more honestly *why* you want to do a thing. If you want to do something in order to please another person or group, and if the doing of it does not please you but you are thinking of doing it anyway, don't do it.

When you please another at the cost of your own integrity, you please no one. For not even the "other"—if they really love you—would want you to do something that made you go against yourself only to please *them*.

If they knew you were going against yourself to please them, what you did would have exactly the opposite effect. It would *not* please them, but, rather, it would make them uncomfortable.

SO HOW CAN I BEST DEAL WITH ALL THE PRESSURES I AM FACING?

Learn to "feel" the difference between "good" pressure and "bad" pressure, between useful pressure and useless pressure.

Useful pressure is the intensification of your

own desire to be, do, or have something that you, yourself, have chosen to be, do or have.

Useless pressure is the anxiety that results from your need to be approved of by someone else.

Never do anything to please another.

THAT'S A PRETTY RADICAL STATEMENT!

It sounds more radical than it really is. There are many times in life when it will please you to please another. In that case, do it. Only when it does *not* please you to please another should you refrain from doing it.

It always pleases you to please another when you and the other share the same self-interest. In other words, when you both want the same thing.

The trick is to look at what another person wants, and what you want, and examine those things closely. If you examine them *very* closely, you will be surprised how often you will find something in what the other person desires that you desire also.

It is in finding those areas where you hold mutual interest that the elimination of "bad" pressure is accomplished. When you find common ground, you lose grounds for anger.

Remember that always: *When you find common ground, you lose grounds for anger.*

All of a sudden it becomes clear to you that you are doing something, not just because someone else wants you to do it, but because *you* want to do it, for reasons that benefit *you*.

GIVE ME AN EXAMPLE.

Easy. Suppose your mother asks you to baby-sit your little brother.

UGH.

Yes. You feel that way because it's something that you don't want to do.

DUH . . .

But what if you found a reason to want to do it?

YOU MEAN, LIKE, GETTING PAID?

That's one reason. There could be others. Payment comes in many forms. As does profit.

Remember that always: *Profit comes in many forms.*

You may choose to quote this wisdom later, in conversations with your parents and others, when they begin discussing "success" with you.

But, getting back . . . supposing you've been trying to prove to your mother that you're responsible enough to stay out after a certain hour, or to take a job in town next summer, or whatever.

Now you've got a different agenda. You say to your mom, "I'm going to show you how well I can do this, because I want you to 'get' that I can do other things just as well. I want you to know that if I can be trusted to take care of my little brother, I can be trusted to take care of *me*."

WOW. I NEVER THOUGHT OF *SAYING* ANYTHING LIKE THAT! COULD YOU COME INTO MY HOUSE AND JUST LEAVE SOME LITTLE NOTES AROUND FOR MY MOM?

That's funny, but you know, later on we're going to be talking about some real good ways to communicate with parents, and leaving little notes in which you put your feelings is one of them.

But, going back, do you get the example? There are others I could give you.

I THINK I SEE WHAT YOU'RE SAYING.

Almost everything you do, you do because at some level you can see your own interests being served. It is not just about the interests of the person "making you do it."

Now the seeing of your own best interest in the interests of another *is a miracle that changes everything*. It eliminates all sense of pressure and resentment, replacing it with a sense of joy in the doing of what you are doing.

Another word for this is Love.

7

Being What You Choose

 IS MY LIFE CONTROLLED BY FATE?
—Patrick, 18

 IS OUR DESTINY PLANNED OUT FOR US?
—Mariana, 17, Florida

Absolutely not. Never. Your life, Patrick, is controlled by you. That is what I meant when I answered the question at the beginning of this book about who gets to do or be what. Do you remember the question? Here it is again. . . .

"HOW DO YOU DECIDE WHO GETS TO BE ALANIS MORISSETTE OR MICHAEL JORDAN, AND WHO GETS TO LIVE REGULAR LIVES?"

And here is the answer I gave:

"I do not decide who gets to be Alanis, and who gets to live regular lives. You do. You are making those choices right now. The problem is, you don't know that you're doing it—or how."

Actually, this same question was asked by a number of you. Here's the way someone else put it:

WHEN YOU CREATE PEOPLE, HOW DO YOU DECIDE WHICH TALENTS TO GIVE EACH PERSON? WHAT MADE YOU GIVE CELINE DION HER GREAT VOICE, RATHER THAN MAKING HER A GOLD MEDALIST FIGURE SKATER OR DOCTOR? —*Paul*

This might be one of the most important things that I've come here to tell you, so let me repeat what I just said.

I do not make those decisions, Paul. You do.

Think of it this way. You are creating yourself anew in every single Moment of Now. You are painting a portrait of yourself. The canvas on which you will paint is Life Itself. The skills, talents, and abilities, characteristics, physical qualities, and outer circumstances are the colors you will use. I supply the canvas, you choose the colors.

THAT CAN'T BE TRUE. I WOULD HAVE CHOSEN TO HAVE A VOICE LIKE CELINE DION. WE *ALL* WOULD! OR THE ABILITY TO HIT HOME RUNS LIKE MARK MCGWIRE. OR ACTING TALENT OR LEADERSHIP SKILLS OR WRITING ABILITY, OR *SOMETHING* OTHER THAN BLAND NORMALCY.

There is no such thing as "bland normalcy." There are only people who *settle for that.*

Everyone is special, *everyone* is extraordinary, *everyone* is talented and skilled and has abilities unique to their purpose for coming here.

WHICH IS?

You come into your life intending to experience your Self in particular ways, for particular reasons. You are a Consciousness and an Awareness before you come into this life. That is, you exist as an entity, as a Being, prior to your birth.

After deciding how it is that you would like to use your life, and what you wish to understand and experience, you pick the exact and perfect people, places, and things with which to accomplish that.

YOU MEAN WE PICK OUR OWN PARENTS?

Yes. And your parents pick you. This is, at a very high level, a joint decision. In fact, it's true of the coming together of all people.

No one meets anyone by accident.

WHY WOULD I HAVE PICKED PARENTS WHO ABUSE ME?

Each soul picks the right and perfect people, places, and events with which to create the opportunity to fulfill the soul's agenda, which is different in every case, and, so, cannot be commented on in general terms.

Perhaps a soul is seeking to experience itself as that quality of divinity known as forgiveness. Or perhaps it is seeking to acquire the compassion to help other people who have been abused, later in life.

There are countless reasons why the soul might call a particular circumstance or person to itself.

THEN THERE'S NO SUCH THING AS A "CHANCE ENCOUNTER"?

There is not. Do you imagine that a universe which designs something as intricate and undup- licated as a snowflake produces something as random as a "chance" encounter?

I THOUGHT THERE MIGHT BE "RANDOM CHANCE" IN THE UNIVERSE, YES.

There is not. Everything is occurring in per- fect order. If there was "random chance," then things would be out of control. What kind of a God would allow things to get out of control?

SO YOU ARE CONTROLLING AND CREATING EVERY- THING THAT IS HAPPENING?

I did not say that. I said that I would not allow things to get *out* of control. Yet I am not doing the creating. You are.

THEN COULDN'T I CREATE THINGS GETTING "OUT OF CONTROL"?

If you are creating it that way, then they are *not* getting out of control. Anything you do deliberately—and all creation is a deliberate action at some level of consciousness—cannot be said to have placed things "out of control."

OKAY. SO HOW AM I DOING ALL OF THIS CREATING AGAIN?

The power to create works in you in three ways:

> In your thoughts
>
> In your words
>
> In your actions

Every thought you have is creative. Every word you speak is creative. Every action you take is creative. These are the Tools of Creation, which I have given you, and they are very powerful.

This is what I earlier described as Original Power. You were not born with "Original Sin," but with Original Power.

SO I GET TO BE LIKE ALANIS BY THINKING THAT I'M GOING TO BE LIKE ALANIS? BY TALKING LIKE ALANIS? BY ACTING LIKE ALANIS?

No. If you do that, you will simply be a copy of Alanis, and a very bad copy at that, because there is only one Alanis, just as there is only one you. Yet, you can be what you see Alanis being—and that is what you may wish to emulate.

Look at what you see this young woman being. Do you see her being talented? Strong? Self-confident? Honest? Authentic? Courageous? Impactful? Successful and happy? What are the States of Being that you see her displaying in, as, and through her life?

Do not look at what she is doing, look at what she is being, because "beingness" leads to "doingness," it is not the other way around. There is something she is being that has allowed her to do all of the things she is doing—and she was being

69

these things *before she was doing any of what she is now doing*.

"Beingness" precedes "doingness" every time—and, indeed, *sponsors it*.

AND HOW DO I GET TO "BE" THESE THINGS?

With every thought, word, and action. These are the tools with which you create States of Being.

If you use them consistently, you, too, can "be" talented, strong, self-confident, honest, authentic, courageous, impactful, successful, and happy.

Whether you are "doing" the thing called rock concerts or "doing" the thing called meeting with your corporate board or "doing" the thing called raising your children, you will *be* the thing called *successful* and *happy* because you have chosen these States of Being, and all the other States of Being that lead to it, and have consciously expressed them in, as, and through you with every thought, word, and action.

BUT HOW CAN I "BE" HAPPY BEFORE I AM? HOW CAN I "BE" SUCCESSFUL BEFORE I ACTUALLY AM? I DON'T UNDERSTAND. HOW CAN I "BE" TALENTED,

**STRONG, SELF-CONFIDENT, OR ANY OF THOSE THINGS,
IF I'M *NOT*?**

Start *thinking that you are*. Start *talking as if
you are*. Start *acting as if you are*. You do not
have to "be" a thing before you can think, talk,
and act as if you *are* that.

**THEN I'M NOT REALLY THAT. I'M JUST MAKING
BELIEVE.**

Exactly. Did you hear what you just said? You
are "making believe." And when you make
yourself believe it, you experience it!

Many people have said that "seeing is believing." What I am telling you is that "believing is
seeing."

What you believe, you begin to see in your
reality.

WHY? WHY DOES THAT WORK?

Because thoughts, words, and actions are
energies. They move and create other energies.
They set things into motion.

Everything that has ever happened, everything that has ever been invented or produced

71

or accomplished, began as a thought in someone's mind. Then it became words that were spoken. Finally, it became actions that were taken. These are the three Tools of Creation, and there are no others.

Here is the greatest secret of life: I have given you tools with which to create the reality of your dreams. *I do not choose* who does what, who gets what, and who gets to be what. *You do.*

IS IT REALLY THAT SIMPLE? I MEAN, *REALLY*?

There is no mystery to it at all. I have just laid it all out for you.

So what you choose to create in your life you must think about. And think about it *positively*. Do not think, "Oh, I could never do that. I could never be that," because *that will become your reality.*

What you choose to create in your life you must talk about. And talk about it *positively*. Do not say, "I'm not sure," or "maybe," or "wouldn't it be great IF . . . ?" Rather, say . . . "It will be great WHEN . . . !"

And what you choose to create in your life you must act on. And act on it *positively*.

Do not fail to act, but positively *be* it!

8

What Teenagers Want Most

During my travels around the world I came to realize that there are so many things that young people are saying they want—and very few older people listening to them. Here is what I heard when I listened to you:

You want, in the words of Robert Kennedy, *to seek a newer world*, to create a place where there is no more irrelevance, pointlessness, or hypocrisy, and no more separation between us—which means there would be no more anger between us, no more quarreling and fighting between us, no more wars between us.

You want a place where we share and share alike; and we don't steal from each other, because we don't hoard from each other; and we don't grab from each other, because we don't withhold from each other; and we don't hurt each other, because we know that when we do, we only hurt ourselves.

You want a place where we don't hide from each other and lie to each other and run from each other, but run *to* each other and hold each other and make love to each other the way we were meant to—all the time, anyplace, anywhere—because all of *life* is about making love. To everything.

And I'm not talking about sex here. The people who think that I've just made a reference to sex here are living in stereotypes, in predictable, half-century-old ideas. Teenagers understand that I'm talking about *love* here.

I'm talking about living a life that is *loving* to *life*, not hateful to life; that embraces life, does not shove life away; that honors life, does not dishonor it with every action and thought and word; that supports and sustains life, does not take from it, and *take* from it, and TAKE from it until it's destroyed.

I'm talking about living in a way that *gives life* to life, not that sucks all the life *out* of life.

Now living that way may sometimes involve sex, but sex isn't the point of it all. It's only part of it all. Love is the point of it all. We will be talking about sex in this book, because people have so many hang-ups about sex that it's unbelievable. But there is a much larger statement made about Life in this book.

Love is the point of it all.

Okay, so there it is. Now you don't even have to finish the book. It's all right there in that sentence. *Love is the point of it all.*

But you already knew that, didn't you?

Yeah, you already knew that.

So the point of this book is not to tell you something that you don't already know. The point of this book is to take you *back* to what *you do know*, and give you *the courage to stay there, to live from there*. Even as you grow older and become what other people call "adults." Even as you become part of the world you wish to change. *Especially as you become part of that world.*

75

Those are the things that young people told me they want—and one thing more. The most important thing of all. I saved it for last, *because* it is so important to all of you—and, in truth, to all people everywhere. This was the item at the top of your list.

Freedom.

You want freedom.

? **WHY CAN'T PARENTS JUST LET US BE WHO WE ARE, INSTEAD OF TELLING US WHO THEY WANT US TO BE?**

—Sandra, Bloomington, Illinois

It is the most difficult challenge faced by parents everywhere to stop directing the lives of their children.

Parents have such high hopes for their children, such dreams and aspirations.

YES, BUT THESE ARE *THEIR* HOPES AND DREAMS, NOT *OURS*!

Yes, but it is not easy for them to let go of these when they feel so deeply about you, when they love you as much as they do, and especially when they honestly think that they do know what's best for you!

It is also not easy to do when these very same parents are the ones who have been counted on, depended upon, for all these years to provide guidance and direction for you.

It's a tough role to give up. It's a difficult assignment to end.

SO WHAT ARE YOU SAYING, I JUST HAVE TO "PUT UP WITH IT"?

You can help your parents, first, by understanding how difficult it *is* for them to "let go," and by giving them time to adjust to their new role as advice-giver or listener, rather than direction-giver.

Hopefully you will never stop going to your parents at times for advice, because their advice will often be very good.

The switch from giving "directions" to giving "advice" or pointing you back to your own inner wisdom and truth can be made by parents fairly early in the lives of their children—usually earlier than they think. This is especially true if they have raised their children with love and not fear.

Children who are *afraid* of making mistakes must be watched more closely for a longer period of time. Children who *love* to make mistakes can be "cut loose" at a much earlier age.

HOW CAN YOU "LOVE" TO MAKE MISTAKES?

Simple! When you know that you are going to be rewarded for them!

All children (and all people) actually *are* rewarded for every "mistake" they make. Their reward is what they learn from what has occurred.

OH, GREAT. SOME "REWARD."

Wait a minute. *This is no small thing.* What you learn from your life can bring you incredible benefit.

Scientists understand this, which is why research scientists actually *relish* their "mistakes." An experiment "gone bad" is actually an experiment that leads to *good*.

This is also true in every walk of life. The rewards of every action and decision are enormous, and you begin to really appreciate them when you add them up, when you consider them in this light.

There is not a person on Earth who has

not concluded at some point that what they once considered a "huge mistake" turned out to be, actually, a big blessing.

You, too, will one day see that, ultimately, there is *no such thing as a mistake*.

WELL, THAT'S AN INTERESTING POINT OF VIEW.

It's a "point of view" that can change your life.

Consider this: "Mistake" is just another word for "failure," and failure does not exist. It is one of those misunderstandings I was talking about earlier. It is an illusion.

It is impossible to fail at anything, and saying that something was a "mistake" is just announcing a point of view.

If you see a "mistake" as a step along the path by which you get to where you wish to go, then you will not see it as a "mistake" at all. You will see it as progress.

It will, therefore, be perfect, and you will be grateful for it. You might even choose to celebrate it!

In the best of companies, owners and managers *celebrate* the "mistakes" of their employees, sometimes even throwing a party, or giving the employee a bonus.

"Now we know what we don't want to do, and how we don't want to do it," they say. "This is a huge step toward guaranteeing our success!"

Firms with such a policy produce employees who innovate, who stretch, who are not afraid to make decisions and to take risks, and that is how the greatest gains are made—which, of course, good management understands perfectly. Good management also understands that *all error is progress*.

Good parents understand the same thing.

Remember this always: *All error is progress*.

Children who are rewarded—held, hugged, squeezed, kissed, and otherwise positively reinforced—when they make childhood "mistakes" will *love* to make "mistakes." They will also grow into adults who *love to live life*.

They will not be afraid of their own shadow (nor of anyone else's). They will grow in confidence and in their ability to step out on the edge and confront the challenges of life, turning those challenges into opportunities to experience their own magnificence.

BOY, DO I NEED YOU TO TALK TO MY PARENTS!

Are you kidding me? *I am*.

WHY CAN'T I STAY OUT AS LATE AS I WANT? WHAT'S WITH "CURFEWS"? I DON'T GET IT! WHY AM I BEING TREATED LIKE A CHILD? WHY CAN'T I BE GIVEN THE FREEDOM TO GO WHERE I WANT TO GO AND DO WHAT I WANT TO DO, AS LONG OR AS LATE AS I WANT TO DO IT?

—Brian, 16, Indianapolis, Indiana

Freedom is not something that others give you. Freedom is the essence of Who You Are. The words Freedom and God are interchangeable. God *is* Freedom. Freedom *is* God.

Your soul is an individualized aspect of divinity. It is the essence of who you are. If your soul could be described by a feeling, it would be Freedom.

And also, Love.

But Love, of course, *is* Freedom, expressed. And Freedom is Love expressed. And Love expressed Freely is what God is!

Are you seeing the picture here? *It's all the Same Thing.* You are simply giving different names to the One Thing there is.

COOL, BUT YOU'RE NOT ANSWERING MY QUESTION.

I'm laying the groundwork.

You're asking why your parents can't give you the freedom that you want, and I'm saying that you already have that freedom, because it is inherently who and what you are.

If there is anything that you are not being or doing, like staying out past curfew, it is because you have chosen not to.

I HAVE CHOSEN NOT TO? THERE'S A SWITCH. IT'S MY *PARENTS* WHO ARE STOPPING *ME*.

No, it's you who are stopping yourself. Do you think there are no children who have not remained out longer than their parents wanted them to? Or, for that matter, run away from home at 14, 15, or 16 and never gone back?

YEAH, AND MOST OF THEM WERE PROBABLY SORRY ABOUT IT, TOO.

That's true.

SO YOU'RE NOT SAYING HERE THAT I SHOULD DELIB-ERATELY DISOBEY MY PARENTS, OR RUN AWAY FROM HOME, ARE YOU?

Of course not. I'm saying that you should exercise your freedom to do as you choose—but to notice that *you are doing the choosing*.

I'm saying that you may exercise your freedom to honor your parents' curfew or not.
But if you choose to honor it, *do not say that
your parents are making you.* You are doing
what you are doing for your own reasons, not
theirs.

Remember the baby-sitting example?

Human beings often seek to make other
people responsible for their choices and their
experience. Freedom is understanding that *you*
are making the choices and *you* are creating the
experience.

In other words, you are doing what you are
doing in order to get something out of it.

YOU MEAN, LIKE A PLACE TO LIVE? YOU MEAN,
LIKE PEACE IN THE HOUSE, WITHOUT LOTS OF
SCREAMING AND HOLLERING? YOU MEAN, LIKE
AVOIDING BEING GROUNDED? IS THAT WHAT YOU
CALL "FREEDOM"? DOING THINGS TO AVOID BAD
OUTCOMES? THAT DOESN'T SEEM LIKE FREEDOM
TO ME. THAT FEELS LIKE COERCION.

Nobody can be "coerced" to do anything.
They can only feel as if they are.

THAT'S NOT TRUE IN THE REAL WORLD. IN THE
REAL WORLD, PEOPLE ARE FORCED TO DO ALL
KINDS OF THINGS AGAINST THEIR WILL.

I understand that you see it this way. In truth, all anyone is ever doing is making choices.

BUT THERE ARE TIMES WHEN YOU *HAVE* NO CHOICE!

There are *never* times when you have no choice. That's what I'm telling you. If you make the choice to do something that is not your parents' choice, you may have to face particular consequences, but that does not mean you had no choice.

Your choices always reflect your desires and your values. That is always true. Your choices reveal all of your ideas about what you want and who you are. There's no question about that. Yet your choices do not announce that you don't have any freedom, but exactly the opposite.

Remember this always: *Every act is an act of self-definition.*

For every example you can give me of someone who has "had to" do something, I can find someone who has done it the opposite way.

There are parents who have deserted their children, rather than raising them. They are not raising their children "because they have to." Your parents are not raising *you* "because they have to." The moment you understand this you will see your parents in a different light.

There are children who have run away from their parents, rather than obey them. They are not obeying their parents "because they have to." *You* are not obeying your parents because you have to. The moment you understand this you will see your life in a new light.

There are people who have chosen death, rather than a certain kind of life. They are not doing what they are doing "because they have to."

WE'VE HAD THIS EXCHANGE EARLIER. YOU'VE SAID THIS BEFORE.

I am saying it again because this is a very empowering place of clarity at which to arrive. Once you arrive at this place, once you understand this, everything changes—including how you experience yourself and everyone else in your life.

Remember this always: *Nobody does anything they don't want to do.*

OKAY, OKAY, BUT YOU NEVER ANSWERED MY REAL QUESTION. WHY DO PARENTS HAVE TO IMPOSE A CURFEW IN THE FIRST PLACE? OR LIMIT MY FREE-DOM IN *ANY* WAY? WHY CAN'T THEY JUST GET OUT OF MY WAY?

Your parents are not *in* your way. They are *paving* your way. They are smoothing what could be a very rocky road. They will not always be there to do this road-paving for you. But while they are, look to see if it serves you to have them do it.

YOU'RE STILL NOT ANSWERING MY QUESTION! WHY DO THEY HAVE TO "PAVE MY WAY" BY *LIMITING ME*?

All right. Let's see if we can get into the head of your parents here.

Moving into the fullest expression of all that you are right here, right now, in this very instant, could be a very overwhelming experi-ence. That's why I've given you *a lifetime in which to do it.*

Have you ever been overwhelmed? There may have been weekends when you were over-whelmed simply with the amount of your *home-work*, yes?

Well now, imagine if all the choices in life were placed before you right here, right now—all the choices about beingness, about values, and about every important life experience. Do you think you might go into a little bit of "over-whelm"?

If you did, it would be because you don't remember fully who you really are. *Your life is the process by which you remember that.* If you "live life a little at a time" you will be able to better take in all the data that life is throwing at you.

I know that you can understand this. If you were baby-sitting that little brother of yours we were talking about earlier, there are things that you would and would not let that child do, right?

BUT I AM *NOT A CHILD ANYMORE.* I KNOW WHAT I NEED TO KNOW. AND BESIDES, HOW WILL I EVER GET TO KNOW WHAT I DON'T KNOW IF I'M NOT ALLOWED TO SEE WHAT I DO KNOW?

You will not. You cannot ever get to know anything if you are not allowed to.

THAT'S MY POINT! THAT'S WHAT I'M TRYING TO SAY!

Conversations with God for Teens

I understand. You will not learn anything about life if your parents won't let you. What parents are trying to do, of course, is help you sidestep having to learn "the hard way." They mean well. But if they are not careful, they will surround you with rules, restrictions, limitations, regulations, and guidelines that do not allow you to confront any real or important choices in life—much less deal with the results that come from you making them.

The question for parents is not whether to allow their children to confront and make their own choices, but how many, how fast, how soon?

This can be a decision made jointly with children.

BUT MY PARENTS DO NOT MAKE THESE DECISIONS "JOINTLY" WITH ME. THEY ISSUE COMMANDS. THEY LAY DOWN RULES. THEY GIVE ORDERS.

Effective parents do not. Effective parents respect the fact that their children are simply younger human beings, with all the inherent rights (and desires) of humans everywhere.

Yet maybe your parents have only their own childhood experience to go on. Maybe they had rules laid down by their parents. Maybe you can help break the chain by talking and listening to them.

 HOW COME ADULTS WANT RESPECT BUT DON'T GIVE IT BACK?

—*Peter, Moscow, Russia*

Some older adults do not know how to give respect to their children. The idea of "respecting" a human being who is so much younger than you, and to whom you gave life itself, is almost foreign to them.

These are usually people who confuse "respect" with "fear," instead of associating "respect" with "love." They respect others— people who are older, stronger, more powerful by means of their position, whatever—because they fear what could happen if they do not. People who respect others because they love them find it easy to respect their children.

Effective parents walk in that understanding and operate within that framework, issuing few, if any, arbitrary rules and orders, but rather, offering to their children (in an age-appropriate way) the chance to create *with* them the conditions of the life that they are living together.

SO WHAT DO I DO ABOUT *MY* PARENTS?

Sit down with them and have a conversation with them like the conversation we are having here.

THAT WON'T WORK. THEY WON'T LISTEN. THEY NEVER LISTEN. THEY DON'T WANT TO LISTEN TO ME. ALL THEY WANT IS FOR ME TO LISTEN TO *THEM*.

If that's true—if that's really true—then show them this. Say, "Mom, Dad, I don't want to be disrespectful, and I don't want to get into another argument with you, but would you be willing to read something for me?" Then give them this book, opened to this page.[2]

AND IF *THAT* DOESN'T WORK?

Then exercise your freedom. Use your Original Power. You can ignore your parents and accept the consequences, or you can avoid the consequences by not ignoring your parents. It's your choice.

SOME CHOICE.

It is the same choice you will have for the rest of your life. Nothing is going to change. Only the "players" in this "drama" will be different. The script will be the same.

Always you will face a choice between what you desire and what you are willing to be, do, or have in order to experience what you desire. *This is the process by which you will define yourself.*

All of your life you will define yourself—you will decide, and reveal, Who You Are—by your desires. Did you know that? If you want to know how evolved people are, look to see what they call "happiness."

You further define yourself by what you are willing to be, do, or have in order to experience what you desire.

So what you are going through with your parents is merely a training for a process that you will go through for the rest of your life.

This can be a joyful process if you truly understand what is going on, for this is the process of *freedom being expressed.*

9

Sex

WHY DO MY PARENTS FREAK OUT ABOUT SEX? MY GOD, THEY *FREAK OUT*.

—Susan, 14, Spartanburg, South Carolina

Mostly, your parents "freak out" about sex because their parents "freaked out" about sex. And, their parents freaked out about sex because *their* parents freaked out about sex. It's been going on this way now for hundreds of years.

Not everywhere. Not in all places, nor in all cultures. There are cultures on your planet in which sex is not seen as anything shameful or embarrassing or as something to be concealed and not talked about and to be "done" in hiding.

Yet in the largest number of places it is seen as exactly that.

Most humans are even ashamed of their own bodies. Or they are simply scared of them. And so they make absolutely certain that they are covered up, and then they actually *pass laws requiring them to be*.

And why? Because most humans are afraid of what will happen if they see each other naked. They imagine that they will run rampant with unresolved desires, fill their mind with unhealthy fantasies, unleash animal urges that they will be unable to control. (Despite the fact that in sunbathing resorts and nudist camps nothing of the sort happens.)

BUT WHY? HOW DID IT GET TO BE THAT WAY?

Somewhere along the way, many humans convinced themselves that most anything "good" is "bad" for them, and that it is in combating their desires, and denying them, that they please God.

Somewhere along the way, they created the idea that passion for earthly things denies them heavenly things. And so they embraced *renunciation* as a spiritual practice. (This is the practice of denying oneself earthly pleasures in order to concentrate on what is "really" important—which some said had nothing to do with being happy here, but, rather, earning happiness in heaven—or, as some Eastern mystics shaped it, becoming "enlightened.")

RENUNCIATION IS NOT A GOOD PRACTICE?

You cannot renounce Who You Are in order to BE Who You Are. The first step in being holy is being whole.

Remember that always: *The first step in being holy is being whole.*

When you deny a part of yourself, you deny an aspect of yourself that I created. This is as much as saying that I didn't know what I was doing. Or, worse yet, that I knew exactly what I was doing and now *demand that you overcome it.*

OR USE IT IN A DIFFERENT WAY?

Renouncing something is not using it in a different way. It is not using it at all. Sex—and the beauty of sex, and the passion of sex, and the excitement of sex, and the wonder of sex, and the pure, unbridled joy and *fun* of sex—is something that I have given you. To renounce it is to renounce me.

Therefore do not renounce sex, nor any of the good and wonderful and fun things that I have given you in life. Simply renounce any addiction you may have to them. This is different from a requirement to live without them. This is a noticement *that you can*.

SO BECAUSE HUMAN BEINGS THOUGHT THAT GOD WANTED THEM TO RENOUNCE SEX, THEY HAVE TURNED IT INTO A SHAMEFUL THING?

To put it simply, yes. There was a time when humans considered their sexual desires and activities to be natural, joyful functions of life. There was no shame or embarrassment around them.

Then your cultural teachings changed that, making you think that to engage in sex openly and playfully and joyfully was "indulging your lower nature," and was unpleasing to God.

Some groups and religions even taught that the only way to holiness, or enlightenment, was to abstain from sex altogether.

Others saw that if everyone did this, the human race would disappear, so they taught, instead, that sex was a "necessary" part of life if new children were to be created, but that "procreation" was its sole purpose and only real justification.

This meant that sex for reasons other than making babies was not okay. Birth control was not okay, sex outside of marriage became not okay, and sex among younger people (who were not in a position to become married *or* raise children) was *absolutely* not okay.

Having intercourse for reasons of pure passion and simple physical pleasure, to say nothing of burning true love and an urgent desire to unite with the beloved, was considered a violation of the "sacred nature" of sex.

Today, some of that thinking has changed, and there is a more lenient attitude toward sex in many societies. Still, it can be difficult to capture the joyfulness if there must be "sneaking around" and "hiding" going on.

Of course, part of what makes sexual expression joyful is a willingness to be responsible with these energies. This is true of all of life.

When human beings act irresponsibly, in any area of their behavior, they can bring all sorts of worries, complications, and unwanted consequences into their lives, and into the lives of others.

There are three Core Concepts of Holistic Living (which we will discuss later), and responsibility is one of them. When human beings act responsibly, they can act joyfully.

Yet even with today's more open attitudes, it is still true that sex—this natural joy of all human beings—was so condemned in the past that today in your society many people still cannot bring themselves to use the proper name for certain body parts—and they certainly don't allow others to see them. Simple nakedness is now called "immodesty."

Put plainly, many people are ashamed of themselves. Human beings have become ashamed of their own bodies.

And when it comes to their children, a lot of parents do, indeed, "freak out" about sex.

I MEAN, *REALLY*. MY FATHER HAS NO PROBLEM WITH ME WATCHING A MOVIE WITH BLOOD AND GORE AND VIOLENCE AND PEOPLE GETTING BLOWN AWAY RIGHT AND LEFT, BUT A MOVIE WITH NAKED PEOPLE MAKING LOVE? NEVER!

Yes, this is a reflection of the attitudes of your society, and it is a big part of what creates your environment, in which sexuality is REpressed and violence is EXpressed.

? **WHICH BRINGS UP ANOTHER QUESTION. HOW COME I HAVE TO PAY ADULT TICKET PRICES AT THE MOVIES AT AGE 13, BUT I CAN'T SEE AN "R" MOVIE? THAT'S STUPID.**

—Karus, 14, Ashland, Oregon

You're being treated as a child with regard to content, but as a full-fledged adult when it comes to the theater owner's pocketbook.

RIGHT!

Given your society's preoccupation with making money, the tilt of this law in the direction of the business owner is not surprising—nor is the contradiction that it requires. Humans will never stop their contradictory behaviors until they alter their priorities.

SO WHAT *IS* THE PURPOSE OF SEX?

—Richard, 14, Miami, Florida
(Also asked by many others.)

You must declare that for yourself. Everything in life has the purpose you give it. I do not give things in life a purpose. I have only given a purpose to life itself. It is the purpose of life to provide you with an opportunity to announce and declare, create and experience, express and fulfill Who You Really Are.

You are made in the image and likeness of God. God is the Creator. That is the image in which you are made. That means that *you* are Creators.

If I told you what to create, and how to create it, then you would not be creating at all. You would simply be obeying.

Remember this always: *Obedience is not creation*.

And so it is that I give you gifts, and you decide what to do with them.

Life is your greatest gift. It exists as an opportunity for you to create and recreate yourself anew in each golden moment of Now in the next grandest version of the greatest vision ever you held about Who You Are.

Sex is another gift. Expressed and experienced responsibly, it is one of the most joyful, exciting parts of life.

Allow me to repeat, so that there can be no mistake about it, that responsible sex, with every health aspect understood, and every consequence considered, and every care taken and every joy expressed, is what is being discussed here.

SO WHAT IS THE "GREATEST VERSION OF WHO WE ARE" WITH REGARD TO SEX?

As I said, you get to decide that. Some people believe that the purpose of sex is to share love and to celebrate life. Some believe it is to simply satisfy a basic physical instinct. Others, as I mentioned, say that its main purpose is to make babies. You may agree with any of these points of view, or you may create your own.

 WHY AM I A LESBIAN? —*Jenny, 16, Miami*

You are a lesbian, Jenny, for the same reason that you are right-handed or left-handed, have brown eyes, or own any other personal characteristic that makes you "you."

Human genetics produces all of your individual physical characteristics, long before you are born. This is very natural, you are very natural, and the way you are is perfect for you.

I love you just the way you are, because the way you are is perfect for you. And that means it is perfect for me.

Go now, out into the world, and *celebrate* who you are. Celebrate your skills and your talents, your hopes and your dreams, your passions and your visions.

Celebrate all that makes you one with the Universe, and all that makes you unique.

Yet when I say "celebrate," I do not mean be insensitive to others. Celebration is not about pushing something in another's face, or deliberately making people uncomfortable.

Celebration is about the peaceful acceptance and the happy experience and the joyous expression of who you are. A celebration is always a contribution. You can tell if what you are doing is a celebration by looking at what it contributes to yourself and others.

So celebrate, and *contribute*. For as you contribute to life, life will contribute to you, and out of what you contribute, life will provide you the grandest experience of Who You Are.

Remember that always: *Out of what you contribute to life will life provide you the grandest experience of Who You Are.*

[?] I'M CONFUSED AND SCARED ABOUT WHAT TO MAKE OF MY NEWLY FOUND SEXUAL IDENTITY. I HAVE JUST CONCLUDED THAT I AM GAY. HOW CAN I PRESENT THAT TO THE PEOPLE I LOVE?

—Tommy, 18, Mobile, Alabama

Tell them the truth. If you are afraid to tell them, then say that. Tell them that you are so afraid of their disapproval that you don't feel you can be honest with them anymore. Tell them that there are certain things that you are afraid to discuss with them, and ask them if there is something they could do or say to help you not be afraid anymore.

If they cannot do this, or if your fear does not go away, then feel the fear and tell your truth anyway. Tell them lovingly what it is you wish to communicate about your sexuality, and ask them for their advice on how you might best deal with your experience.

If you have become aware of experiencing physical attraction to persons of your own gender, and you share this with your parents, give them room for their honest reaction and try very hard not to make them wrong for that reaction, just as you hope that they will not make you wrong for your choices and decisions.

Tell them what you wish to say and ask for their love, letting them know that they always have yours, no matter what. Model for them what you hope to experience *from* them. In short, do unto others as you would have it done unto you.

This may not be easy, especially if their reaction is very negative, personally attacking, or condemning. Still, remember that all attack is a call for help.[3]

WHY CAN'T I JUST HAVE SEX AND HAVE IT BE OKAY WITH EVERYBODY? WHAT'S THE BIG DEAL?

—Claudia, 16, Perth, Australia

Nothing you do will ever be okay with everybody. "Everybody" is a large word. The real question is, can you have sex and have it be okay with *you*?

And the question right behind that would be: What could cause it to be okay with you?

IT IS OKAY WITH ME! IT WOULD BE FINE WITH ME! IT'S JUST NOT FINE WITH EVERYBODY ELSE! THAT'S THE PROBLEM!

Why is it a problem?

BECAUSE MY PARENTS WOULD KILL ME, FOR ONE THING.

They would not kill you, and they would probably not even be surprised. What you are saying is that they would not approve.

YES, THAT'S WHAT I'M SAYING. DUH . . .

Why do you think your parents would not approve?

BECAUSE THEY THINK THAT SEX IS BAD. WRONG. SHAMEFUL. WHAT*EVER*!

That may be true, but if you become a keen student of the human race you will observe that people often hold views that are different when they consider them as individuals from the views they hold as a group.

MEANING?

Meaning that it is possible your parents, *individually*, don't hold many or any of the ideas about sex held by society as a whole.

THEN WHY DON'T THEY WANT ME TO EXPERIENCE IT?

Maybe because they simply feel it's too soon.

TOO SOON? HOW SOON IS "TOO SOON"? I'VE READ THAT IN SOME SOCIETIES PEOPLE DO IT WHEN THEY ARE 12!

There is no prescribed time for sexual initiation and sexual activity. It is different from culture to culture and from person to person.

WELL, I THINK I'M READY.

Really? Have you looked closely at all the possible outcomes? Have you explored, really explored, the consequences of deep love entanglements? Pregnancy? Sexually transmitted diseases—including AIDS?

Do you know all that you believe you need to know on these subjects? If you're not sure, talk about them with your parents. If you are sure, still talk with your parents. Share with them what you understand.

Talk to them about AIDS, HIV, and everything you know about that. Ask about anything you don't know. If your parents don't know either, find the answers together.[4]

Explore the various methods of birth control. Do you know everything there is to know about all of this?

Talk with your parents about all of this.

ARE YOU KIDDING ME? THERE'S NO WAY WE CAN TALK ABOUT THIS.

That may not be as certain a thing as you think.

IT'S CERTAIN, BELIEVE ME.

Then have them read this book.

HERE WE GO AGAIN.

I'm serious. Have them read this book.

Then if they still won't talk with you about it, tell them you are on the verge of making some decisions about your sexuality and that you'd rather do it with their good input than without it. And tell them that you do not consider "orders" good input.

YOU'RE SOMETHING, YOU KNOW THAT? YOU THINK I CAN SAY THOSE THINGS TO MY PARENTS?

If you can't have an honest conversation with your parents, what is the point of *having* parents? *Ask them THAT.*

PHEW . . .

Yup. "Phew" is right.

Tell them why you want to have sex, how you hope to deal with it in your life, the values that you have created around all that, and then ask for their honest, caring, loving input.

And don't be shocked if your parents surprise you.

They may be more than willing to talk, they may be totally able to "hear" that edicts and

orders don't work anymore, and they may have
greater understanding and empathy about your
feelings and desires than you think.

**YOU SAID ON THE FIRST PAGE OF THIS BOOK THAT
I CAN HAVE AS MUCH SEX AS I WANT, EVERY DAY
OF MY LIFE, AND IT WOULD BE VERY OKAY WITH
EVERYBODY. WHAT WERE YOU TALKING ABOUT?
THAT DOESN'T SEEM LIKE WHAT YOU ARE SAYING
HERE.**

I said that first you must understand what
sex is—and that it may not be what you think.

**I THINK I HAVE A PRETTY GOOD UNDERSTANDING
OF WHAT SEX IS. MAYBE NOT FROM *EXPERIENCE*,
BUT I'VE HEARD ENOUGH TO KNOW WHAT'S GOING
ON.**

You may know enough about intercourse to
know what is going on, but do you know
enough about sex?

If you do, then you know that you are
already "having sex" every day. Sexual energy is

exchanged between people from the moment they meet.

All of you are energy transmitters, and you are sending your signals in a 360-degree circle all around you. These rays extend from you into infinity. They crisscross energy rays from other beings and from other things, forming a never-ending web of intersecting emanations that physically impact the space in which they exist, setting up very particular vibrations.

Everything that exists sends out these emanations.

It is this "vibe" that you feel, and to which you react, when you find yourself in any particular space. You can "feel the vibe" as soon as you walk into a room or enter any place. Likewise, you can feel the vibe *shift* as soon as the emanation from any other being shifts—to say nothing of the emanations from a whole group of beings.

People react to these emanations, animals and plants react to these emanations, the earth itself reacts to these emanations.

The entire Universe reacts to these emanations.

The entire Universe IS these emanations. That's what the whole system IS. It is what holds everything within the system together. It is what sends information to the system about the system. It is the essence of everything.

The spectacular process through which this essence emanates from, to, and through everything in existence is called S-E-X, or . . . Synergistic Energy eXchange.

IT'S LIKE . . . *THE MATRIX*!

Yes. And as in the movie, *it is also an imagined reality*. The only thing different is that there is no sinister force behind it, no colony of artificial intelligence, no army of robots.

The imagined reality of your matrix is being created by you. You are the creator and the created. Your matrix is the combined energy field put into place by the lot of you. Its effects are localized by the power of this force field when it is intensified in any particular time and place.

This force field cannot be seen by most people, although it can be felt by everyone, and nearly everyone can describe how it feels at one time or another, in one way or another. Those who are highly sensitive feel the force field constantly.

Students on the road to mastery have learned

that they are both *feeling* and *creating* it, and they are in the process of remembering how to use this force in their lives.

Masters are those who have come to a deep awareness of all this, and it is in and from this essential essence that they live and move and have their Being.

When you experience S-E-X with a Master, you know it.

I GOT IT. BUT I THINK YOU KNOW THAT THIS IS NOT THE KIND OF SEX THAT I WAS TALKING ABOUT.

It is all the same thing. We are simply talking about different expressions of the same energy.

When you understand this, when you realize that you are "having sex" in every single moment, then you become much more aware of both the energy you are sending out and the energy that you are receiving.

You begin to create your Sending Energy deliberately, in a particular way. After you do this consistently for a while you are said to have "charisma."

SO JUST EXACTLY HOW DO I DO THIS?

It is done with such a simple instrument, such a simple tool. The tool is called "mood."

The mood you are in is the mood you bring into a room and can easily affect the mood in that room. Thus, you can be said to be recreating it anew. Everything changes because you walked in.

Now the Magic of Mood is something that most people do not understand. You have an opportunity right now to come to an understanding of it that can change your whole life.

WILL IT IMPROVE MY ROMANTIC LIFE? THAT'S WHAT I'M TALKING ABOUT HERE!

Believe me, this has everything to do with the kind of synergistic energy exchange you are talking about. In *any* kind of S-E-X, mood is everything.

Now the Magic of Mood is that it can be creative, and does not have to be reactive.

Most people think that mood is their reaction to something outside of themselves—something that exists or has occurred. This, they say, has put them in a certain mood, or even "ruined their mood."

Those who know the Magic of Mood understand, however, that mood need not be only a "reaction," it can be a "creation." That is, *you can decide ahead of time what mood you want to be in,* before you have any idea of what conditions exist or what events are going to occur in a particular time and place.

By choosing your mood ahead of the moment rather than after it, you impact the moment in an incredible way. You begin to *create* the conditions that exist and the events that occur.

Your mood changes the moment, rather than the moment changing your mood. Your mood changes people, rather than people changing your mood.

Suddenly, with regard to how you are experiencing your life, *you are at cause in the matter.* You are no longer "at the effect" of life, but "at cause."

This simple switch can alter every waking moment.

THAT IS GREAT. THAT IS JUST, LIKE . . . WOW. I NEVER CONSIDERED THAT. I NEVER THOUGHT OF THINGS LIKE THAT. I MEAN, THAT WAS A PRETTY FAR-RANGING DISCUSSION CONSIDERING WE STARTED OUT TALKING ABOUT MAKING LOVE.

We never stopped talking about "making love."

Remember this always:

Love is not measured by how many times you touch each other, but by how many times you reach each other.

WHOA.

Yes, whoa.

NOT ALL TEENAGERS FEEL THAT SEX IS IMPORTANT AT THIS STAGE IN THEIR LIVES. I, FOR ONE, THINK THAT WAY TOO MUCH IS MADE OF IT. I HAVE NO INTENTION OF HAVING SEX UNTIL I GET MARRIED.

That's very okay. Have you decided why?

SURE. BECAUSE I THINK THAT SEX IS A SACRED PART OF THE HUMAN EXPERIENCE AND IS ONLY TO BE SHARED INSIDE OF THE SANCTITY OF MARRIAGE.

Who told you that?

MY MOM. BUT I AGREE.

Cool.

I'VE NEVER HEARD OF A GOD WHO SAID "COOL" BEFORE.

God speaks to people using language that is natural for them. Don't you ever say "cool"?

YEAH.

Cool. So do I.

SO I'M RIGHT ABOUT SEX AND MARRIAGE?

It is not a question of being "right," it is a question of "what works" for you. You are always defining yourself, by every thought, word, and action.

YES, BUT WHAT DO YOU THINK? WHAT DOES GOD SAY?

This might be a good time to tackle the whole subject of God, and how it is with me.

10

God

 WHO ARE YOU? —*Brigit, 13, Oslo, Norway*

Who am I not?

I DON'T UNDERSTAND WHAT THAT MEANS.

It means there is no one, and nothing, that I
am not.

YOU MEAN, YOU ARE EVERYTHING, AND EVERY-ONE?

That's what I mean, yes.

EVEN BAD PEOPLE, AND BAD THINGS?

There are no "bad" people and no "bad" things, only people and things that you have called "bad."

THAT'S THE SAME THING.

To you, it is. To me, it isn't.

NOW WHAT DOES *THAT* MEAN?

It means that we have different values. It means that we have different understandings. It means that you have made judgments, and I don't make judgments.

GOD DOES NOT MAKE JUDGMENTS? I THOUGHT THAT'S WHAT GOD *DID*.

Well, the human race has been thinking that for a long time, but it's not true. It's one of those misunderstandings I've been talking about. It's

117

an illusion. The illusion of judgment. Followed by the illusion of condemnation.

It has been written: Judge not, and neither condemn.

? YOU MEAN, YOU REALLY DO NOT JUDGE? YOU FORGIVE EVERYONE, NO MATTER WHAT THE SIN? —*Lily, Miami, Florida*

I do not forgive anyone. That is the first thing you must understand about me. I will not forgive you, ever, for anything that you do.

Once you are clear about this, you will have a new understanding of God, and you will be able to interact with me in a whole different way.

I do not forgive anyone because there is nothing to forgive.

YOU MUST BE KIDDING!

No. Forgiveness is only required when someone has been hurt or damaged. You cannot hurt or damage God.

I CAN'T HURT YOU? DOESN'T IT HURT YOU WHEN I SIN?

No. Any more than it "hurts" you when you see a toddler "sin" by doing something he is not "supposed" to do. Do you feel "damaged"? Do you feel "hurt"?

NO . . .

Of course not, and neither do I. You cannot injure me in any way. I am All, I have All, I will always be All. There is nothing I need or want, nothing I require to be "happy." I do not need you to do, or not do, something, I do not need you to be, or not be, something, I do not need you to have, or not have, something.

I do not need you to worship me, or fear me, or love me.

BUT YOU DO NEED US TO OBEY YOU, RIGHT?

There is nothing I need from you, therefore, nothing I am asking of you, therefore, *nothing for you to obey.*

Do you think I am up here making up rules for you to follow, regulations for you to adhere to? *You* are making those up.

Since I cannot be injured in any way, I have no reason to ever feel angered or upset. "Forgiving" you for something you have done is unnecessary, because nothing you have done could ever injure me, and in the absence of injury there is no need for retribution or "justice."

Even your own courts have held that you must prove injury before you can seek justice. If the court holds that you have not been injured by another, that other will not be punished "just for the hell of it"! Now if your own human courts would not do this, why would I?

BUT WHAT ABOUT IF I *DO* DO BAD THINGS TO OTH-ERS? MAYBE I CAN'T HURT YOU, BUT I SURE CAN HURT OTHER HUMAN BEINGS—AND I HAVE. THAT'S WHAT MOST PEOPLE FEEL THEY NEED TO BE FOR-GIVEN FOR.

Yet you do not need to seek that forgiveness from me. I have not found you as having done something "wrong" to me, so I have no reason to forgive you.

I understand why you have done everything you have ever done in your life. I know what you were thinking, and why you did it.

When you understand why someone did something, even if you don't agree with their reason, it becomes very difficult to remain angry with them. In my case, I never became angry in the first place.

I understand too much. I know too much. Anger is not something of which I am capable. The level of my comprehension does not allow it.

I STILL FEEL BAD ABOUT HURTING OTHERS.

Then seek forgiveness *from those others*. And seek forgiveness from yourself.

THERE ARE SOME THINGS FOR WHICH I JUST CAN'T SEEM TO FORGIVE MYSELF.

Do you want to know how to be able to do this?

YES! **TELL ME HOW, YES!**

Forgive the same offense in others. Forgive the same faults, the same foibles, the same offensive character traits, the same sins in others that you see yourself having and committing.

WILL THAT WORK?

It is the magic formula. You heal your heart when you heal the heart of others.

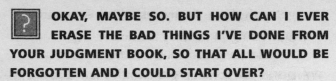 OKAY, MAYBE SO. BUT HOW CAN I EVER ERASE THE BAD THINGS I'VE DONE FROM YOUR JUDGMENT BOOK, SO THAT ALL WOULD BE FORGOTTEN AND I COULD START OVER?

—*Ayla, 13*

My wonderful Ayla, there IS no "judgment book." That's what I'm trying to tell you all here!

I am not Santa in the Sky, making a list and checking it twice so that I can find out who's naughty and nice. That is not Who I Am. That is not what I do.

It may be a surprise for most humans to learn that there is no such thing as right and wrong. There is only what works and what doesn't work, given what it is that you are trying to do.

HOW CAN THAT BE? ISN'T KILLING WRONG? ISN'T CRUELTY WRONG?

If killing is wrong, if cruelty is wrong, what about wars, what about hitting someone who has broken into your home and is taking your baby?

THAT'S DIFFERENT. THAT'S SELF-DEFENSE.

Oh, so you mean that there *are* situations in which killing and cruelty are not wrong.

WE DON'T CALL SELF-DEFENSE KILLING OR CRU-ELTY. WE CALL IT SELF-DEFENSE.

Changing your terminology does not change your actions. It merely justifies them.

ARE YOU SAYING THAT WE SHOULD *NOT* KILL OR INFLICT INJURY IN SELF-DEFENSE?

That is not what I am saying, and that is for you to decide, not me. You are creating your own reality with such choices. These and other decisions that you make about your species and how all of you will live together is what creates the world as you know it.

It is not for me to decide how you are to create that world, then see if you will do it and punish you if you do not. I have given you free will to create the world of your highest imagining. If this is the highest imagining that you can come to right now, then so be it.

The point being made here is that Absolute Right and Absolute Wrong do not exist. A thing is "wrong" only because you *say* it is wrong, and a thing is "right" for the same reason. And human beings change their minds about what they say is right and wrong all the time, depending upon the circumstances.

WHAT'S WRONG WITH THAT?

Nothing. That's the point. There is nothing "wrong" with changing your mind about what's "right" and "wrong," because that's what *works*, given what you declare that you wish to do.

If you declare that what you wish to do is live in peace and harmony, then saying that it's "wrong" to hurt or kill someone in self-defense might not work for you.

One day it may come to pass on Earth that it will *not* work to kill or hurt someone in self-defense, but that could only happen in a very highly evolved society in which it is understood that the Self does not need to be defended, because it cannot be hurt, damaged, or destroyed.

This is not currently your understanding, and what works for you—your ideas about right and wrong—will always be a reflection of your current understanding of things. What you call "right" is merely the best way that you currently know how to achieve what it is that you declare you wish to experience.

SO "RIGHT" AND "WRONG" ARE A CHANGING THING?

Yes, changing and shifting from time to time and place to place.

It may not be "wrong" to drive a car at 120 miles an hour if you are trying to win the Indianapolis 500, but could be "wrong" if you are trying to get to the grocery store. It all depends on what you are trying to do.

If you are driving west in the United States, and you wish to go to Seattle, it is not "morally wrong" to turn south and head for San Jose. It is not a question of "right" and "wrong." It is a question of what gets you where you say you are going.

WOW. NOW I GET IT!

Right and wrong, therefore, do not exist as absolutes, but only as momentary assessments of What Works and What Doesn't Work. You make these assessments yourself, as individuals and as a society, given what you are wishing to experience and how you see yourself in relationship to everything else that Is.

WHAT DOES THAT MEAN?

If you see yourself as One with all others and with everything else that Is, you will have one set of ideas about What Works and What Doesn't Work in your thoughts, words, and actions. If you see yourself as separate from all others and from everything else that Is, you will have another set of ideas.

Everything depends on what you are seeking to accomplish (put more broadly, what you understand to be the Purpose of Life), and how you experience your relationship to all that exists (how you define Who You Are).

AND THIS IS WHERE BELIEFS COME IN.

Exactly. Your beliefs about that produce one set of standards, someone else's beliefs about that will produce another. Society's beliefs as a whole will produce a cultural story that will play itself out again and again throughout the course of your collective history. And your collective history has proven that.

DON'T MANY OF US LOOK TO OUR RELI-GIONS TO GIVE US OUR HIGHEST BELIEFS?

—*Josh, 18*

Yes, and your religions have taught you about separation, need, superiority, failure, judgment, and condemnation. These are the beliefs that keep you stuck in a system of Absolute Right and Wrong and in a cultural story of separation that is killing the lot of you.

SINCE WE'RE ON THAT SUBJECT, HOW IS IT THAT A GOD OF MERCY CAN BE SUCH AN ISOLATIONIST AND SO INTOLERANT TO OTHER VIEWS? HOW CAN A GOD OF INFINITE MERCY CON-DEMN ANYONE FOR ANYTHING? WHY CONDEMN FOR ETERNITY THOSE TRANSGRESSIONS THAT ARE MOMENTARY?

—*Scott, 18, Sacramento, California*

Scott, I am not an isolationist, nor am I intolerant. I think that you are talking about a different God here. Perhaps it is the God about whom you have been taught. That God is largely a figment of your collective imaginations.

And I also—as I just said a moment ago—do not condemn anyone for anything. I have been saying this over and over again to the human race through many sources for many years.

Many of the people to whom I have given this truth have passed my words on to the world, including spiritual leaders such as Pope John Paul II.

At a papal audience in Rome on July 28, 1999, the Pope declared:

"Eternal damnation is never the initiative of God, it is the self-imposed punishment of those who choose to refuse God's love. . . ."

That statement by the Pope was accurate. What it means is that I will not ever undertake to punish you, but you *can* punish *yourself*. You can *create your own hell*.

Self-punishment is simply your decision to judge yourself, or to deny My existence and My presence, and thus separate yourself from me.

THE POPE SAID "ETERNAL DAMNATION IS NEVER THE INITIATIVE OF GOD"?

Yes. He also made some other very courageous pronouncements about heaven and hell during that same period in July of 1999. You may check your own newspaper accounts of all this.

Those press dispatches reported his statement that heaven is not a place, but an intimate relationship with God that can be experienced partially on Earth.

Also reported in the press was the Pope's statement that the idea of heaven as a place in the sky came from metaphorical biblical language contrasting the dwelling place of humanity and the dwelling place of God.

But the Old Testament makes it clear that God "cannot be enclosed in heaven," that God hears human prayers, intervenes in human history, and that, "through grace, believers can ascend" to God's presence, the Pope said.

Finally, regarding hell, Pope John Paul II said that eternal damnation *is not a punishment inflicted by God from outside*. It is an internal state of separation from God.

And then, Scott, came the Pope's most astonishing statement of all. Whether or not any human beings are in hell "remains a real *possibility*, but is *not something we can know*," he said.

Until now, no Pope and no Christian teacher of any renown has ever come even close to suggesting that there could be anything but absolute assurance about souls being in hell, which these teachers declared to be the place of "eternal damnation." Now, here comes the spiritual leader of the largest Christian church on your planet to declare that he can't be sure about that.

Other religions, too, have changed their tune and softened their official rhetoric about hell and damnation in recent years, and these newest statements from the world's spiritual leaders offer important signs that your worldview about me is changing.

Now you can stop living your lives in constant "fear of the Lord," and have a friendship with God instead of a "fearship with God." This is not a small shift. This is not a tiny alternation. This changes everything.

IN WHAT WAY?

Our relationship can at last be one of love, not terror.

The exciting thing about this is that when you stop fearing me, you can stop fearing each other. You can begin to believe the highest truth about God (which is that I would never hurt anyone) and the highest truth about life (it is eternal, love is all there is, and there is enough of God, and of life, and of all the stuff of life for everyone), the highest truth about each other (you are all one) and the highest truth about your own blessed being (its purpose is to evolve forever, and it cannot be destroyed under any circumstances at all).

This changes how you relate to me, how you relate to yourself, and how you relate to each other.

It changes the world.

 WHY ARE THERE SO MANY WARS OVER WHO HAS THE RIGHT AND CORRECT RELIGION?
—Park, Seoul, South Korea

Most of your Earth religions believe that there is only one way to God, and that their way is this one way. They believe this—and teach it—so fervently that they feel themselves to be superior in my eyes. They have accepted as real the illusion of superiority.

Many of them also believe that they must convince others to believe as they do, and that in doing this they are meeting their responsibility to me.

Finally, some religions and their followers believe and teach that persons of religions other than their own are my enemies, and so must be converted, removed, or eliminated.

These thoughts and ideas have produced justifications for ethnic cleansing, religious intolerance, and so-called "holy wars."

As I said earlier, these ideas spring from a belief in an entire set of illusions around which humans have built their understandings of life, their philosophies, their religions, their political systems, and their economic systems. The illusion of superiority is but one of them.

These illusions are not real, but they have been made to seem very real because of the power that humans have given them.

NO WONDER THE WORLD IS THE WAY IT IS.

Yes. It exists inside of a belief system of fear, insufficiency, and false superiority. Most of your worldwide institutions—not just religion, but politics, economics, education, and social constructions of every variety—exist inside this paradigm, operate in this setting.

That is why there are so many wars over who has the "right" and "correct" religion, the right and correct political system, the right and correct economic system, and the right and correct amount of the "stuff" on Earth of which humans think there is "not enough."

It is the struggle to gather the "stuff of which there is not enough"—into which category, sadly, you have also put God's love—that produces wars.

In the future you may add water to this list.

WHAT?

Because of the way you have lived, you may create a situation in which water will appear to be part of "the stuff of which there is not enough." In many parts of your world, that is already becoming true. And so, you may have, in the twenty-first century, what you will call Water Wars.

Remember how you labeled your biggest battles World War I and World War II?

YEAH . . .

Well, now you may very well have Water War I and Water War II—if you ever get that far. With today's technology, one war may end everything.

MAN, NICE PICTURE, NICE PREDICTION.

I said, "may." You can still avoid this. Just as you can still avoid not having enough clean air, not having enough usable topsoil, not having enough trees to create oxygen, and not having enough covering over your planet to protect it from global warming.

You can avoid all of these things. There is still time. And now you are here. You have arrived on the scene. And maybe you will choose to change things. But do not choose to change things by only changing *conditions*. Work to change conditions, yes, but know that you must also change the beliefs that create the conditions, or sooner or later everything will just return to the way it was.

 WHY DOESN'T EVERYONE BELIEVE IN ONE GOD? —*Peter, 17, Zagreb, Croatia*

Most people do believe in one God. *Their* God. To them, "their" God is the only God, and everyone else's God is a false God. Sadly, this idea has resulted in the killing of a lot of people—in the name of God.

Now, it is natural for people to wish to express themselves in ways that allow them to experience their individuality. That is why people dress differently, comb their hair differently, drive different cars, and live different lives in so many different ways.

The trick here, Peter, is to see if members of the human race can find a way to not let their individual expressions separate them and cause them to feel righteous or superior.

Righteousness and superiority about your expressions of individuality—whether religious, or political, or philosophical, or economical, or social, or sexual—can lead to insane behavior.

In the book *Friendship with God*, I brought the human race a new gospel that would heal the world in two sentences:

We are all one.

Ours is not a better way, ours is merely another way.

I challenge every priest, every minister, every rabbi, every nation's leader, every politician, every economist, and every teacher in every school to stand up in front of those who listen to them this week and preach this gospel. I challenge them to say these fifteen words.

These are fifteen words that would save the world, yet your presidents and your prime ministers, your popes and your bishops, your politicians and your teachers have never been able to utter them.

WHY?

Because there is one thing that human beings will give up everything for. They will give up happiness, love, joy, peace, prosperity, romance, excitement, serenity, *everything*— even their own health—for this.

WHAT? WHAT IS IT?

Being right.

WHAT IS THE ROLE OF RELIGION IN LIFE IF RELIGION IS NOT SUPPOSED TO SAY THAT IT KNOWS THE "RIGHT" WAY TO GOD? DOES IT HAVE A ROLE? *—Monica, 17, London, England*

Religion, as with everything else, plays the role that you give it.

You could give it the role of bringing people closer to God and closer to each other. Right now I observe that, in more cases than not, religion has done the opposite.

In fact, nothing has done more to separate people from each other and from God than organized religion.

I LIKE GOING TO MY CHURCH. I BELIEVE IN MY RELIGION. ARE YOU SAYING THAT I SHOULDN'T?

Absolutely not. I would never suggest that any person give up their religion if they believe in it with all their heart and all their soul, and if their lives are happier because of their beliefs.

WHAT *WOULD* YOU SAY?

I would say, go about living the answers you have, but never stop questioning the answers you are living.

That is the true posture of every seeker, and it is the true purpose of every religion.

I observe that many humans derive great value from religion. Religions, therefore, will always have an important role to play in the human adventure, so long as they open doors, and do not slam them.

WHAT IS THE DIFFERENCE BETWEEN "RELI-GION" AND "SPIRITUALITY"?
—Thomas, 16, Queenstown, New Zealand

One is an institution and the other is an experience.

Religions are institutions built around a particular idea of how things are. When those ideas become hardened and set in stone they are called doctrines and they become largely unchallengeable. You either believe them or you don't.

Spirituality in its freest form does not require you to believe anything. Rather, it continually invites you to notice your experience.

Your personal *experience* becomes your authority, rather than something that someone else has told you.

If you had to belong to a particular religion to find God, it would mean that God has a particular way or means by which you are required to come to Him.

WHY WOULD GOD REQUIRE THAT?

The answer is, I don't. The idea that God has only one way of approaching Her, or one particular means of returning to Her, and that this way and only this way will work, is fallout from the illusion of requirement.

This is another of the illusions of humans, another of those misunderstandings we've discussed. And it has nothing to do with ultimate reality.

I have no need to require anything of you, because I have no need to receive anything from you. Is saying a rosary better than saying the savitu? Is the practice called bhakti more sacred than the practice called seder?

NO. OBVIOUSLY, NO. THEN WHY DO RELIGIONS INSIST THAT THEIR WAY IS THE BEST WAY—NO, NO, THE *ONLY* WAY—TO YOU?

Well, we're going around and around on this now, and it starts to feel as though I am just repeating myself here.

WAIT. TELL ME ONCE MORE. I WANT TO BE ABLE TO GET THIS.

It is helpful for religions to imagine this because it gives them a tool with which to seek, acquire, and retain members—and thus, to continue to exist.

It is the first function of all organizations to perpetuate themselves.

The moment any organization serves the purpose for which it was formed, that organization becomes no longer necessary. This is why organizations seldom complete the task for which they were created.

Organizations are not, as a rule, interested in rendering themselves obsolete.

This is as true of religions as it is of any other organized undertaking. Perhaps more so.

The fact that a particular religion has been around for a very long time is not an indication of its effectiveness, but just the opposite.

 BUT IF IT WEREN'T FOR RELIGION, HOW WOULD WE KNOW HOW TO GET TO HEAVEN?

—Lawrence, 15, Kansas City

In the first place, you cannot *not* "get to heaven." There is no other place to go. Yet, even if there were, and you were looking for "directions" to heaven, religion could be a very confusing place from which to get them.

There are many different religions on the Earth, and each one has its own set of "directions," reflecting its best idea of how "God wants it."

Of course, as has been said here now repeatedly, there is no particular way that God "wants" you to worship God. Nor, in fact, does God need to be "worshiped" at all.

God's ego is not so fragile that She must require humans to bow down to Her in fearful reverence, or grovel before Him in earnest supplication, in order for God to find them worthy of receiving blessings.

What kind of a God would this be?

That is the question you must honestly ask yourself.

You have been told that God has made humans in His image and likeness, yet is it possible that religions have fashioned God *in the image and likeness of humans*?

BUT IF YOU ARE ALL-POWERFUL AND MIGHTY, AND YOU CAN CREATE MIRACLES, THEN WHY DON'T *YOU* TURN NONBELIEVERS INTO BELIEVERS OF YOUR RELIGION?

—Jacques, 16, Paris, France

It would be hard for me to get people to believe in "my religion" because I do not HAVE a religion.

As we've just discussed, everyone would like to think that I have a religion, and that my religion is *their* religion, but the miracle that I have created is much greater than the miracle you wish to attribute to me. The real miracle is that everyone is going to return to me, regardless of the path they take.

They will return to me because *there is nowhere else to go*. I am All There Is. There *is* nothing else.

I tell you again, there is no hell. There is an *experience* of hell, which is separation from me, but you can end that experience whenever you wish—either in this life, or in the next.

I am the Alpha and the Omega, the beginning and the end, the All In All. You cannot avoid your happy destiny—but you can postpone it.

Yet all it takes to speed your journey is a yearning sincere and true. In that moment of yearning, I will be there. You do not have to "come home" to me. You will know in that moment that I have always been with you.

Just as I am here, in this book.

HOW COULD SOMEONE NOT BELIEVE IN YOU, GOD? —*Jennifer, 19*

Everyone has free will, to believe or not believe what they choose. Most people's beliefs are based on their experience.

Masters are people who live life the other way around. Their beliefs are not based on their experience; their experience is based on their beliefs.

Masters have turned everything upside down. Or, really, right side up.

It is very okay that some people do not believe in me, Jennifer. Not believing in me cannot cause me not to be.

I am always with you, *believe it or not*.

 WHEN WILL YOU COME DOWN AGAIN? —*Steven*

I never left. Don't you see? I never left! That's the whole point here. Everyone thinks I left, and I never left.

I am here, with you and around you and in you. And when you understand that, you no longer have to feel alone. You no longer have to feel abandoned. You no longer have to feel afraid. And you no longer have to worry about how or whether you can get back to me. I am here. *I never left.*

AND YOU WILL NEVER LEAVE ME, EVER?

How could God leave you? You are too glorious, too wondrous, far too special to ever be left. Indeed, the reason that you *are* glorious, wondrous, and special is that I never left you.

We are One. Do you not believe this? If you do not, then you have misunderstood everything I have ever tried to show you, everything I have ever tried to reveal to you through the process of your life. Yet that process is not over. *It will never be over.*

We have Forever to know and experience the truth of our Oneness.

 WHEN IS YOUR NEXT PROPHET COMING AND HOW WILL I KNOW WHO HE IS?
—*Ashley, 17, New Bedford, Massachusetts*

My prophets are arriving every minute of every hour of every day, Ashley. The dictionary defines "prophet" as "one who utters divinely inspired revelations," and "one gifted with more than ordinary spiritual and moral insight." There are thousands of such people all over the world. You do not have to wait for one to come; you merely have to recognize them when they do.

You also have the option, Ashley, of simply being that yourself.

ME? HOW COULD I BE THAT? I COULD NEVER BE THAT.

Yes, you could. This is a great secret of life. You can all *be* what it is that you are waiting for. And as soon as you choose to be that, your waiting is over.

If you are waiting for love in your life, *be* the love for which you are waiting.

If you are waiting for compassion in your life, *be* the source of compassion for everyone whose life you touch.

If you are waiting for laughter and fun to enter your life, bring that into the room when you *enter* the room.

What you are waiting for will arrive when you arrive with it.

Remember this always:

What you are waiting for will arrive when you arrive with it.

You ARE that for which you are waiting.

I WISH I COULD BELIEVE THAT.

Then DO believe it. For what you believe, you become.

This is something that not many people understand. This is a message that would change the world. You can send this message just by living your life. In this way you will give people back to themselves, by showing them Who They Really Are.

To many of them this will be a great revelation, and you will be a prophet indeed. Not merely in thought, not only in word, but in *deed*.

 HOW DOES IT FEEL TO BE YOU? WHAT DOES IT FEEL LIKE TO BE GOD?

—*Raymond, 14, Boise, Idaho*

Wonderful! It feels wonderful! All the life in the Universe courses through me, because I AM all the life in the Universe, and it is exhilarating, exciting, and wondrous indeed.

How does it feel to be me? It feels . . . peaceful. There is nothing that I need to be happy that exists outside of me.

The same is true of you.

How does it feel to be me? It feels . . . complete. I am whole, complete, and perfect, just as I am.

The same is true of you.

How does it feel to be me? It feels . . . safe. Nothing can harm me, and I will Always Be, eternally.

The same is true of you.

How does it feel to be me? It feels . . . like fun. I can create and create every moment, and experience in the next moment what I have just created.

The same is true of you.

It is wonderful to be me. And it is wonderful to be You. Because You is who I am, and I am who You are. And could there be anything more wonderful than you? I do not think so.

 WHERE DID GOD COME FROM? —*Ricky, 13*

Everywhere. I came from everywhere. And I AM everywhere right now. There is not a single "where" in which I am not. I am in every "where" there is. Therefore, I am nowhere in particular.

So, that's where I am.

No-where.

Or, if you split the words differently . . .

Now-here.

? ARE YOU LISTENING? HOW COME YOU DON'T SHOW ME ANY SIGN THAT YOU'RE LISTENING TO ME WHEN I PRAY TO YOU?

—*Myron, 13*

Oh, but Myron, I *do* show signs that I am listening to you! You simply do not see them, or you see them but do not believe them. Often, you simply dismiss them.

Sometimes when you are praying, your heart will beat faster. Sometimes you will be filled with a feeling of great peace.

Sometimes you'll feel that you want to weep with joy. Sometimes you will have a sudden experience of "oneness" with everyone and everything.

Sometimes an experience of deep understanding or inner awareness or absolute forgiveness for yourself or another will come over
you. These sensations and more are signs
from me.

Sometimes you will feel nothing at all, experience nothing at all. Yet even this is a sign from
me. It is what you could call The Emptiness, and
it is here, in fact, that I reside.

It is from The Emptiness that all wisdom will
come and all healing will orginate. It is from the
void that I have come, and to the void that I will
always return. And your mind can go there, too,
if you will let it.

Why would you want to go to the void?
Because that is where peace will be found. That
is where wisdom will be found. That is where I
will be found, waiting for you.

The void is that place where all thoughts,
all fears, all sorrows, all anguish, apprehen-
sion, misunderstanding disappear. It is the place
where the mind can quiet itself at last, and be at
rest.

You can go there by many paths.

Taking a walk alone. Riding your bike or
cycle. Listening to your CDs. Floating on a
water raft.

Some people use meditation or prayer.

So do not avoid the void. Learn to love the emptiness. This is the Inner Space of Divinity within you.

Fear of the void is very natural, because it feels like nothing. That is, like no thing at all. But do not fear. This is where your true self will be found.

For you are not a thing. You are no thing.

Every "thing" that you think that you are, you are not. The "things" of life, including your very body, are merely tools with which you can experience Who You Really Are. And the first thing you will discover as you use these tools is that you are not these tools, but, rather, the *user of them*.

This will change everything in your life.

HOW? I HEAR THOSE WORDS, BUT I DON'T UNDER-STAND THAT.

You are not your body. Your body is something you have, it is not something you are. And it is not indestructible. *You* are, but your body is not.

Most people have a feeling of indestructibility, especially when they are young, when they are teenagers. It feels as though nothing can hurt them, nothing can harm them, there is nothing they cannot do. *And this is true!* But it is true of their spiritual selves, not of their physical selves.

When you understand this, you actually take care of your body better than you did before. You understand that it is something that you have been given—like everything else in your life—to use temporarily. It is a gift. It is not you. It is a gift *to you*. And you begin to treat it as such.

You begin feeling the same way about relationships. You see all other people in your life as gifts (which is what they are), sent to you to help you recreate in each moment the Divine Being that you choose to experience in, and as, your Self.

Finally, you also come to clarity about the physical possessions in your life as well. You begin to understand that you really have no "possessions" at all, but merely hold stewardship over certain "things" for a little while. If you take good care of them, you can truly enjoy them, and experience that part of your Self that you know as joy.

Yet, then there comes a time when you easily let them go, knowing that "there's more where that came from"—and that you are *not* that.

You are *not* that money, or that job, or that car, or that beautiful house in the country, or any of that "stuff" that you have accumulated. That is "that," and you are "you." And you will be "you" with or without "that."

This is a great awakening. You begin living your life in a new way. You cease the endless effort to accumulate more and more of "that," and you begin the spiritual quest to experience more and more of "you." More and more of Who You Really Are.

? **I'VE READ THE *CONVERSATIONS WITH GOD* BOOKS AND I KEEP HEARING THAT PHRASE "WHO YOU REALLY ARE" USED. BUT WHO AM I, REALLY?** —*Sayaka, 18, Tokyo, Japan*

Who You Really Are is a blessed being. You are not a "thing," nor are you any of the "things" that you have. You are a spiritual being, and it is in the experience of "being" that you will find your greatest joy.

In one word, the being you are is Love. You are that which Love is. That is why, when you are "being" that, you are the happiest you could ever be.

And that is why, when you are not allowed to be that, or not allowing yourself to be that, you are the saddest that you will ever be.

And nothing else will matter. Not what you do, not what you have, and not who you are "in the world." None of it will matter.

Love, of course, is another word for God. The two words are interchangeable. This means that Who You Really Are is me. You are an aspect of Divinity, experiencing your Self.

HOW COME IT DOESN'T FEEL LIKE THAT? HOW COME IT FEELS A LOT, SOMETIMES, LIKE I'M BUMBLING THROUGH LIFE, AND OFTEN AM NOT HAPPY?

Because you have forgotten that you know Who You Really Are and what you're doing here. You may think that you are your "things," and that when you don't have those "things" you can't be happy.

You may think that you are your school, or your job, or your friends or your money or car, or your appearance—the way your body looks—and that if these "things" were taken away from you, you would disappear.

This is the time of your life when you are fighting to create your own identity, and if you are not careful you may identify with these "things" rather than with your True Self.

You may think that you are the color in your hair, or the clothes that you wear or don't wear, or the car that you drive, or the group that you hang with, and that all these "things" *make a statement of Who You Are.*

Yet, if you think this, it will not be surprising if you are often unhappy, because these things have nothing to do with displaying or experiencing your True Self—and *that is what you came here to do.*

These things may be signs of youthful rebellion, but they are not signs of truthful revealing of the innermost part of you.

The trick is to have fun with these things. Do not confuse them with Who You Are, but simply have fun with them. Yet always remember that it is no fun to hurt yourself, no fun to damage yourself, no fun to *hide* Who You Really Are behind a mask of indifference or anger, or a facade of hostility and disaffection.

If you have frustrations with life and "how things are," choose to express them in positive ways that help others change their belief systems, so that the conditions you deplore eventually disappear.

Try not to judge or condemn the people and circumstances that you see filling the stage of life. Rather, write a new play, and become both its director and its star.

11

Success

? I FEEL LIKE I NEED TO BE SUCCESSFUL—AT
EVERYTHING. MY PARENTS SEEM TO DES-
PERATELY WANT THAT. BUT WHAT IS "SUCCESS"?

—Sam, 15, Palm Springs, California

You've asked the question of the century,
and only you can answer it, Sam. Yet that in
itself is an important revelation. *Only you can*

answer the question, Sam. So do not let other people answer the question for you.

Much of your world works within what could be called, in the English language, the "3 P's System," in which it is agreed that the biggest measures of success are Productivity, Popularity, and Possessions.

Under this system, the person who does the most things, has the most people looking up to them, and owns the most stuff, wins. You have heard the joke, "He who dies with the most toys wins." In the lives of so many members of your species, that is not a joke at all.

Are Productivity, Popularity, and Possessions your definitions of success?

I DON'T KNOW. IT SOMETIMES SEEMS THAT THEY SHOULD BE. IT SEEMS AS IF THAT'S WHAT THE WORLD WANTS. MY PARENTS SEEM TO WANT THAT, TOO.

If you choose these definitions, you may have to spend your life attempting to do and have more and more.

Money will be very important to you because it will be a measure of how much *productivity* you have been responsible for, and of how many *possessions* you can acquire, and, to no small degree, how much *popularity* you achieve.

You should know that this can lead to endless and insane competitions—not only with others, but with yourself. You may feel that you have to show *increased productivity* to be seen as worthwhile.

If you get C's in school, you'll be pushed to get B's. If you get B's, someone will want you to get A's. If you get two A's, they'll want you to get four. It never stops, it never ends, always there is the pressure to produce more, more, *more*.

(Some parents even reward their children with more and more *possessions* if they *produce* more and more A's—thereby cementing the link between production, possessions, and "success.")

This emphasis on productivity—that is, on what you are *doing* rather than what you are *being*—can place incredible strain on both individuals and companies, as well as the resources they use.

THAT HASN'T SEEMED TO MATTER TO TOO MANY COMPANIES OR PEOPLE SO FAR.

That is why they have created in today's world merely a modern version of what their ancestors created in the past. If you follow this path, you will opt for *quantity* rather than *quality* as a measure of success in your life—and *that choice will give your life its meaning.*

WELL, I DON'T CARE MUCH ABOUT HOW MUCH I "PRODUCE," BUT I DO WANT PEOPLE TO LIKE ME.

If you imagine that Popularity is the definition of success, you will spend your life seeking the approval of others. The fact that you may lose your Self and your individuality in the process will not matter to you. What remains of you will be "popular," and that limited part of you will have achieved what you have chosen to call "success."

(Some politicians fall into this category, as do some entertainers, who have given up their real thoughts about things, or their real artistry, in order to create and hold their audience.)

IS IT NOT OKAY TO AT LEAST WANT A FEW NICE THINGS?

Desiring objects is a perfectly normal and healthy aspect of life. Yet if you imagine that Possessions are the definition of *success,* you will seek to acquire as many of the "good things" in life as you can—the biggest house, the flashiest car, the best seats at the ballpark—and you will make sure that others know that you have done so.

You will ignore the old saying among your people that "the best things in life are free," and you will work hard all your life to obtain enough money to acquire these glittering physical possessions. Then you will say that your life has been a "success."

THAT DOESN'T SOUND LIKE ME. NONE OF THIS SOUNDS LIKE ME.

Well, then, Sam, you can decide that there are other measures of success.

SUCH AS?

Such as doing something that makes your heart sing! Something that you can get "lost" in for hours. Something that you would do *for nothing*, without ever *worrying* about how much you're getting paid. It's like, *"Just give me a chance to do that."*

YESSSSS! NOW *THAT* SOUNDS LIKE ME!

So how about defining "success" as doing what you love?

MY FATHER WOULD SAY, "YOU CAN'T MAKE A LIV-ING DOING THAT."

Well, you're invited to be one of the coura-geous ones. Someone who has chosen to make a life, rather than a living.

WOW.

Yes, wow.

And that's what success should feel like. Suc-cess should feel like wow, not woe.

You should be able to say, "Wow is me!"

BUT WHAT ABOUT THE BOTTOM LINE? DON'T I HAVE TO FIND A WAY TO MAKE A PROFIT?

Remember what I said earlier?

Profit comes in many forms.

But listen, you can go ahead and make the 3 P's your measure of success. Yet, look to see if it has served others in your world to do that.

Has your species benefited from this defini-tion?

161

NO. AND I DON'T KNOW ANYBODY WHO THINKS SO.

Few people in the world agree *individually* that these are the best measures, but nearly all people in the world have agreed *collectively*. At the very least they have acquiesced, which is the same thing.

WHY DO THEY DO THAT? WHY DO THEY AGREE ON THINGS COLLECTIVELY THAT THEY DISAGREE ON INDIVIDUALLY?

This is what is known as "herd mentality." It is easier to follow the herd than to move in the opposite direction. The fact that the herd is heading for a cliff is irrelevant—if it is even noticed.

CAN WE STOP THE STAMPEDE?

Yes, actually, you can. That's why it was said at the outset that this book has come to end hopelessness.

The first thing you can do is redefine yourselves as individuals. The second thing you can do is redefine yourselves as a society. And a third thing you can do is redefine "success."

You can give life a new purpose.

**THAT'S WHAT I WANT TO DO! I WANT TO FIND A
NEW PURPOSE FOR LIFE. I WANT TO CREATE A NEW
DEFINITION OF "SUCCESS."**

Others in your world have done so. You can,
too. And if enough of you do, the whole "system" can be turned upside down.

IS THIS WHAT YOU WANT US TO DO?

There is nothing that I want you to do. I
have no preference in the matter. Your idea that
God has something that God wants you to do
is what has gotten your species into a lot of
trouble.

I do not make demands, I make observations.

Remember that always: *God does not make
demands, God makes observations.*

I have created Life as a process by which you
may do as you choose to do and experience
what you choose to experience. This is what
free choice is all about.

Out of what you choose to be, do, and have,

163

you decide Who You Are. This is what you are doing in every moment.

I have told you this over and over, and I will repeat this to you often, so that you will always remember it—and thus, remember Who You Really Are.

Now, if it is *your choice* to "turn the system upside-down," and turn your life around as well, there are ways you can do that.[5]

One of those ways is to change your mind about what you think "success" is. Redefine the "meaning of life." Decide that the purpose of life has nothing to do with the Three P's. Live your life according to the Core Concepts of Holistic Living:

1. Awareness

2. Honesty

3. Responsibility

WHAT DO YOU MEAN BY "HOLISTIC LIVING"?

I mean, living as a whole being. Holistic living is whole person living. It is body-mind-and-spirit living. It is before-now-and-after living.

It is being, completely and authentically, all that you choose to be in this moment, now. It is being aware of what you are choosing to be, it is being honest about it, and it is being responsible for it.

Living this way is another definition of "success." What is interesting is that very often people who live this way *also* achieve greater productivity, popularity, and possessions, but *not because they are trying to do so*. This just happens automatically. It is a *by*-product, rather than the *end*-product, of the process called Your Life, Lived.

12

Love

MY GIRLFRIEND ALWAYS SAYS SHE LOVES ME, BUT I DON'T FEEL THE SAME YET, AND I DON'T KNOW WHY. HOW WILL I KNOW WHEN IT WILL BE THE RIGHT TIME TO SAY "I LOVE YOU"?

—Paul, 18

There is never a wrong time to say "I love you," Paul, nor is there a wrong person to whom to say it.

We'll get more into that in just a minute. Right now, let me answer your question a bit more directly.

It is the "right" time to say "I love you" when your heart speaks the words, not your brain. When you do not have a second thought. Nor even a first. When you are completely outside your thoughts and totally into your feelings.

Remember this always: *Only say "I love you" to another when you are out of your mind.*

HA! THAT'S A GOOD ONE.

I actually meant it quite literally. If you've still got to think about it, don't talk about it. Yet love, love, love *everyone*. Silently. In the stillness of your heart. Allow the whole world to feel that love.

Soon you'll find, as you give your love to everyone, that you desire to express your love in particular ways with particular people, based on the way that you are feeling.

You will experience three expressions, in particular, which will define your relationships. Your species has come to call these "eros," "phileo," and "agape." These are being loosely defined in your day and time as romantic love, brotherly or family love, and universal love for God and for all humankind.

These three "kinds" of love have nothing to do with different "quantities" of love, but different "varieties" of love. And these different varieties produce different feelings, which produce different ways of showing love.

Love can be given in the same *amount* to everyone, it can be felt just as strongly for a brother as for a husband, or for all humankind. It is not a matter of strength or amount, but of feelings and expressions.

WHAT, ACTUALLY, *IS* LOVE, ANYWAY?

Your poets and philosophers have been trying to define that for centuries. They come very close to the truth when they say that love is transcending the experience of duality.

It is an experience of oneness, of unity, where there is no separation, where separation is unthinkable. The idea of duality becomes the illusion and the idea of oneness becomes the reality.

This is the ultimate reality. This is the way things really are. You are not separate from each other and you never have been. Love is the human urging to prove that, and to experience it.

You know that you are experiencing love—for yourself and for others—when you identify everyone's best interest as One.

THANKS. THAT'S PRETTY INSPIRING. BUT I'M STILL WONDERING, HOW DO I KNOW WHETHER WHAT I'M FEELING FOR MY GIRLFRIEND IS LUST OR LOVE? HOW DO I KNOW WHETHER IT'S JUST SEX THAT I WANT, OR SOMETHING MORE?

When you say "just sex" you make it sound as though this is not enough, that this is somehow "wrong." That is the old mind-set I was just telling you about. Sex "for the sake of sex" is very bad, is not okay. You have shamed yourself for having these desires. You have made yourself terribly wrong. This is what has created a lot of the anxiety around sex, and all of the guilt. Yet this is a natural desire. *I have built it into you.*

OKAY, SO HOW DO I KNOW WHEN IT'S ONE OR THE OTHER WITH MY GIRLFRIEND? LUST OR LOVE?

Look at your motives for wanting to be around her. If almost every time you are with her all you can think of is having sex with her, then see what that says to you. Don't make those feelings "bad," just know that it's what you're feeling. That's where you're at.

Sexual energy and sexual chemistry can be very strong during the teen years. It's also very natural. This does not mean that all you desire with a person is sex, but it does mean that you are wise to check out your feelings further, and to look deeply into what you mean when you say "I love you."

SO WHAT DO THE WORDS "I LOVE YOU" MEAN?

What some people have *decided* they mean is very often much different from what the words *actually* mean. So I understand why you would be confused, and wondering when to use them.

Much of the human race has decided "I love you" means "I am yours. I belong to you." Or, "I own you."

This translates, very soon, into, "I now owe you something, and you owe me something. It is now my job to make you happy, and you must do the same for me."

This is *not* what it means, but this is what

many people want it to mean, need it to mean, and insist that it should mean. That is why so many people want to hear it, and also why it is so difficult for some people to say it—and for nearly all people to live up to it.

SO IF "I LOVE YOU" DOES NOT MEAN THESE THINGS, WHAT DOES IT MEAN?

"I love you" means "the God in me sees the God in you."

I'VE HEARD THAT SAYING BEFORE. ISN'T THAT WHAT THE WORD *"NAMASTE"* MEANS?

It is. That is another way of saying "I love you."

BUT WE THINK "I LOVE YOU" MEANS I'M READY FOR MORE, I'M MOVING TO THE NEXT LEVEL IN OUR RELATIONSHIP; I'M SEEING YOU DIFFERENTLY THAN I SEE EVERYONE ELSE. IT MEANS "YOU'RE SPECIAL TO ME," AND "THERE'S NO ONE ELSE LIKE YOU," AT LEAST NOT FOR ME.

It can mean that, depending upon the kind of feeling you are experiencing. Remember, with love, the *way* you feel, and the way you *show*

how you feel, will differ from relationship to relationship. Yet different *kinds* of feeling should not be confused with different *levels* of feeling.

This idea that you are seeing someone differently is what has caused many difficulties in life, because what humans seem to communicate is that they love one person *more* than another, when what their soul really wishes to communicate is that they love one person in a different *way* than they love another. They have a different *feeling*.

In truth, you were created with the ability to see everyone through the eyes of love.

WAIT A MINUTE. DO YOU MEAN THAT WE'RE SUPPOSED TO LOVE *EVERYBODY*?

You are not "supposed" to do anything. Who would do the "supposing"? Who is issuing the orders? Who is making the demands? The answer is, no one.

So it is not a question of what you are "supposed" to do, but of what you are capable of doing.

You are capable of loving everyone. Equally. Not in the same way, but in the same amount.

Here is a great secret about love.

Remember this always: *Love is not quantifiable*.

Love is not something that you can dole out in different quantities. You cannot love one person "a little" and love someone else "a lot." You either love someone or you don't.

Once again let me say, *how you feel your love for them is another matter*. What *demonstrations* you make of the love you feel will be a reflection of those feelings. But love itself is not quantifiable.

Most human beings imagine that it is, and, in fact, that it *should be*, and this is another big misunderstanding.

I SHOULDN'T LOVE MY MOM MORE THAN I LOVE A STRANGER IN TIBET? I SHOULDN'T LOVE MY GIRLFRIEND MORE THAN I LOVE THE OTHER GIRLS IN SCHOOL?

It is not a question of "shoulds" or "shouldn'ts." Try not to "should" on yourself, and don't let other people "should" on you, either.

It is a question of knowing Who You Really Are and knowing who everyone else really is.

Who you ARE is love. That is who and what you are. It is the energy of which you are made. It is the energy that holds you together.

(Perhaps this is why, when you feel that you are not being allowed to love, it can seem as if you are "falling apart.")

You are the energy of life itself, which is God *actualized*. Another word for this is love.

The words God, life, and love are interchangeable. You are God, which is life, which is love, which is God, which is life . . . and so on.

It is a circle that never ends, and it is all the same thing.

SO THIS MEANS I SHOULD LOVE ALL THE GIRLS IN THE SCHOOL JUST AS MUCH AS I LOVE MY GIRL-FRIEND?

Not that you "should," but that you can.

MY GIRLFRIEND WOULD BE PRETTY UNHAPPY ABOUT THAT.

Again let me ask you to remember that I am not saying "in the same way," or with the same feeling, I am saying "just as much."

All of life is vibration. That is all that it is. That is all that *you* are. It is possible to be in harmony with another vibration, or to be in sync with it.

To be in harmony means that your vibes and the other vibes blend. The vibrations are occurring at the same time in different ways. You are *harmonized*.

To be in sync means your vibes and the other vibes are occurring at the same time in the same way. You are *synchronized*.

This is a very metaphysical way of saying that you can have different feelings of love with different people, and even different feelings of love with the same people at different times.

This explains what most people mean when they say that they love this person "more" than that person. What they are experiencing is that they love them in a different way. The "vibe" is different.

I GET IT.

When you are being, fully, Who You Are, you will find yourself loving *everyone* just as much. You will not love one person "more" than you love another. You will simply show your love in different ways.

This is how parents are, hopefully, if they have more than one child. They do not love one child more than the other. They love all of their children equally. This is how grandparents are with their grandchildren. This is how God is with everyone.

This is called unconditional love.

Actually, love, by definition, is unconditional. Anything less is not love, but merely Individuated Self-Interest. Love is Unified Self-Interest.

It is the experience of the Self when it sees everyone else as part of It. It is when you see everyone else as part of you. It is unity, expressed.

HOW CAN I PRETEND THAT THERE IS NO DIFFERENCE BETWEEN ME AND ANOTHER PERSON, WHEN THERE IS?

No one is saying there is no difference between you and another person. What's being said is that there is *no separation*.

Your little finger is different from your thumb, yet there is no separation. They are all part of the same thing, which you call your "hand" — and *it* is part of the larger thing that you call your "body."

In exactly the same way, humans are all parts, all members, of *my* body. To experience being God once again, all that you have to do is re-member Who You Are! That is, become *members once again* of the Body of God.

Therefore, choosing not to love all people is choosing not to love a part of *you*.

THIS IS ALL VERY INTERESTING ON A PHILOSOPHICAL LEVEL, BUT WHAT DOES THIS HAVE TO DO WITH ME AND MY GIRLFRIEND?

Love *all* people as much as you love your girlfriend, and watch your life change.

Demonstrate your human love in a different way, but love every person in the same amount, and you will change the world.

This is what Jesus did. This is what The Buddha did. This is what Krishna did. This is what Muhammad did.

YES, WELL, I AM NOT A GOD . . .

Actually, you are. That is what I have been telling you. Yet even those whom you would call "ordinary people" did this. It is what Mother Teresa did. It is what Gandhi did. It is what Martin Luther King did.

I AM NOT A SAINT, EITHER.

You are what you say you are. If you say you
are not a saint, then you are not—by your definition. By my definition you are, because I made
nothing but saints.

**SO, DOES THIS MEAN THAT I CAN SAY "I LOVE YOU"
TO MY GIRLFRIEND RIGHT NOW?**

Remember the Three Core Concepts of
Holistic Living that were just mentioned:

1. Awareness

2. Honesty

3. Responsibility

If you walk in Awareness, you will be very
aware of not only what YOU mean when you
say "I love you," but of the current meaning that
most members of the human race place on this
phrase. If you do not mean what you know
THEY mean by these words, look to see if it
makes sense to say them.

Remember this: when you say something,
most people think that you mean what THEY
mean when they say the same thing.

It is rarely true that you do mean the same thing, but most people think that you do. It is important to be aware of this.

Many people already know this. They let other people *think what they want to think* about what is being said, even when they know that the other person is not thinking what they are thinking. This is called "manipulation."

When you deliberately allow another person to think something that you are *not* thinking when you say a thing, it is a form of lying. Many humans feel that it is the worst kind of lying, because you are not actually saying untrue words, you are simply allowing someone else to draw untrue conclusions.

If you walk in Honesty you cannot do this. You cannot say something that you know someone else is likely to misinterpret. Therefore, if you can honestly say "I love you" to your girlfriend and mean what you know *she thinks you mean* when you say it, then by all means say it. If you cannot, then do not.

HOW CAN I KNOW WHAT SOMEONE ELSE IS THINKING?

You might try asking them.

You might also try saying "I love you" and tell

her honestly what that means to you. Clarify the differences between both of your interpretations, if there are any.

> **THE BIBLE SAYS TO LOVE YOUR ENEMIES. HOW CAN A REGULAR PERSON DO THIS? I MEAN, I GUESS I UNDERSTAND HOW SAINTS CAN DO IT, BUT HOW CAN A REGULAR PERSON LIKE ME DO IT?** —*Maria, 14, Madrid, Spain*

The first step in moving to a place of love for everyone—including your "enemies"—is to move to a place of love for yourself. You cannot give to another what you cannot give to yourself.

If you do not love yourself unconditionally, you cannot love another unconditionally.

Remember this always: *You cannot give to anyone what you do not have to give.*

Therefore, love, love, *love* your Self. See your Self as perfect—just the way you are. This is how God sees you.

To have God love you, you do not have to lose weight, change your lifestyle, improve your habits, get better grades, or do or change anything at all. Believe it or not, you are completely lovable just the way you are.

Remember this always: *You are completely lovable just the way you are.*

Knowing this will change your life.

Believing it will change everyone else's.

That's because what you believe, you become, and when you become perfectly Self-loving, you bring your Self, at last, the equipment with which you can love all others, and that can change the world.

WHO WANTS TO "CHANGE THE WORLD"? I'M JUST TRYING TO GET THROUGH THE WEEK HERE.

It is possible to do both at once.

 HOW CAN I LOVE MYSELF WHEN I SEE SO MANY PARTS OF MYSELF THAT I DON'T LIKE?
—*Nicole, Montréal, Québec, Canada*

Consider the possibility that all the things that you don't like are actually the best parts of you.

MY FAULTS ARE THE BEST PARTS OF ME?

Yes. They are your best character traits—but with the "volume" turned up perhaps just a notch too high.

I DON'T UNDERSTAND.

The part of you that others call "spontaneous" is the same part of you they call "irresponsible" when the volume is turned way up.

The part of you that others call "courageous" is the same part of you they call "foolhardy" when the volume is turned way up.

The part of you that others call "confident" is the same part of you they call "egocentric" when the volume is turned way up.

All of your so-called "worst faults" are nothing more than your *highest attributes*, simply turned up too high for the "music" to be enjoyable.

The things that people fall in love with you for are the very same things they might criticize you for if they feel they are getting too much of it.

They will love you for your willingness to make decisions quickly, and yet if you do it too often in too big a way they will call you "bossy."

They will love you for your incredible

problem-solving ability, and yet if you use it too often in too big a way they will say you always want to do things "your way."

They will love you for your keen sense of humor, and yet if you display it too often in too big a way they will accuse you of being "flighty" and "never serious."

It is the same part of you that others are loving or criticizing, depending upon where the "volume" is set.

I NEVER THOUGHT OF IT THAT WAY.

The exciting part about this insight is that it means you don't have to change a thing in order to be lovable.

You don't have to deny a part of yourself, or condemn a part of yourself, or throw away a part of yourself.

You don't have to "make wrong" any aspect of who you are, or try to fix yourself by making it go away.

All you have to do is watch life a little more closely to see which parts of you are appropriate to have "show up" at any given time, and how big you should let that part of you be just then. What "volume" should you set?

Do you understand?

COMPLETELY! YES, I *GET* IT!

Good. It is a great thing to remember. The very things people have made you "wrong" for are the things that they admire in you when they experience them at another time, or at a different energy level.

What knowing this means is that you can love your whole self again, *just as you did when you were a child*. This is a great release. It is a wonderful moment of self-renewal and self-recovery. It allows you to give "you" back to yourself.

WOW. THAT MAY BE, RIGHT THERE, THE REASON I'M READING THIS BOOK. I MEAN, SO I COULD "GET" THAT.

It may be, indeed.

Now here is the trick. The trick is to "walk in awareness." Look to see what each moment offers in terms of a chance to give the gift of who you are.

See what part of your gift, and how much of it, would enliven the moment, or make it somehow better, and see if there are aspects that could be turned down.

And be aware that there are times when the best gift you can give is the space to allow others to give theirs. This means learning how to let someone else "show up" in their best way—even though you may think you can do it better.

Remember this always: *Sometimes the greatest gift you can give is silence.*

THANK YOU. THANK YOU FOR ALL OF THAT. THIS IS TURNING OUT TO BE A GREAT CONVERSATION.

You're welcome. I'm glad we're having it.[6]

? WHY DOES IT ALWAYS HURT SO MUCH TO LOVE SOMEONE? I'M TIRED OF BEING HURT BY SOMETHING THAT WAS SUPPOSED TO FEEL SO GOOD.
—*Tiffany, 18*

It doesn't have to hurt to love someone, Tiffany, but if one confuses "love" with "need," it almost always will.

Many human beings think that love is a

response to need fulfillment. In other words, if you meet my needs, I love you.

I can understand where humans got this idea, since they have been told that this is how God works. You meet God's needs and God loves you. If you don't, then God does not.

This is not how it is with me, but it is how you've been *taught* that it is, and those teachings are hard to shake, and impossible to ignore.

So let's start with them.

God does not need anything from you. I do not need you to worship me, I do not need you to obey me, and I do not need you to come to me in a certain way in order to achieve your own salvation.

WELL, THAT BLOWS THE LID OFF PRACTICALLY EVERY RELIGION ON THE PLANET.

Sorry. That is just how it is!

God is the All-in-All, the Alpha and the Omega, the Beginning and the End, the Unmoved Mover, The Prime Source, and All That Is.

There is nothing that there is that I am not, and what I am not does not exist. Therefore, *by definition*, I need nothing.

Remember this always: *God needs nothing*.

It follows with impeccable logic that if there is nothing I need, there is nothing I am going to punish you for if you don't give it to me. That includes your personal allegiance, the particular way that you worship or come to me, or, for that matter, even admitting that I exist.

I do not need you to recognize that I exist or to pray to me or to have anything to do with me at all. And I will not punish you in the everlasting fires of hell if you do not.

I've already explained this all in chapter 10, but I'm restating it here in case you didn't quite catch the implications of my earlier comments—or couldn't believe them.

Believe them.

WHAT DOES ALL THIS HAVE TO DO WITH LOVE?

Everything. Human beings love the way they love because they think that this is the way that God loves. Human beings think that love is a Godly response to having needs met, and it is not.

Love is not a response, it is a decision.

A man named Scott Peck put that statement in a book called The Road Less Traveled a few years ago, and it was I who inspired him to do it. I am glad that I did because it is an enormous truth that most people do not understand.

Most people think that love is a response, and they gathered this from their misunderstanding of how and why I love you.

I do not love you for what you do for me. I love you because you are.

Simply because you ARE.

Can you understand that? Can you grasp it? My love is a decision, not a reaction.

I THINK SO, YES. BUT DOES THAT MEAN WE CAN'T DO ANYTHING TO EARN YOUR LOVE?

You do not need to earn what you already have.

Does a rose need to earn the rain?

Does ice cream need to "earn" your love?

Ice cream does nothing to earn your love. It just is. Ice cream is what it is, and you love it.

Think of things this way: *You are God's dessert.*

THAT'S CUTE. I LIKE THAT.

Thanks.

Now you know that I love you because you simply are, and require you to do nothing to "earn" my love. I need nothing from you. Let this be your New Model of Love. Love gives of itself *for no reason*. It is not a repayment, nor can it be a bribe for what you hope will come.

True Love is the result of a decision you make about how you are going to be with another person. If it is merely a response to what another person does, it is not love for another at all, but a counterfeit emotion.

When you make a decision to love another person before you have any idea what they might, or could, or will do for you or with you, that is a very high decision. You automatically increase your vibe. I mean that your being actually begins to vibrate at a higher frequency, at a faster speed.

The feeling of love emanates from you, like rays of sunshine. People feel wonderful around you, and so they find themselves feeling wonderful *about* you.

Suddenly, they increase *their* vibes—and then, you could find yourself *in harmony* or *in sync*.

That's when the heart begins to flutter, and the sparks begin to fly. . . .

BUT HOW CAN I MAKE A DECISION TO LOVE SOME-ONE BEFORE I KNOW ANYTHING ABOUT THEM?

Do you love people because of who *they* are, or because of who *you* are?

WOW. THAT'S A GREAT QUESTION.

Indeed. And your answer?

I'VE ALWAYS LOVED THEM BECAUSE OF WHO THEY ARE, I GUESS.

Thanks for being so honest. Now just change your reason for loving them. When you love people because of who *you* are, you demonstrate that you need nothing from them, that your love is not based on what you can get from them.

BUT I DO NEED SOMETHING FROM THE PEOPLE I LOVE. I CAN'T SAY THAT I DON'T, BECAUSE I DO.

No, you don't. You just think that you do.

There is not a single thing that you need from any other person in order for you to be perfectly happy. Indeed, you have been perfectly happy in many moments of your life without ever having even *met* half of the people that you now know.

YES, BUT ONCE I GOT TO KNOW THEM, I COULDN'T LIVE WITHOUT THEM. ESPECIALLY CERTAIN ONES. ESPECIALLY THAT "PARTICULAR" ONE!

This is not true, but if you think that it is true, it will seem true enough for you. It will also lead to your unhappiness. Because first you will convince yourself that you cannot be happy without a particular person, then you will decide that it is not enough just to have that person in your life, you must have that person be in your life *in a certain way.* (They have to be your regular girl or boy friend. They have to be "hooked up" with you.)

After that you will decide that in order to be happy you must have that person in a certain way *a certain amount of the time*—like, every free moment they have.

Soon, you will imagine that in order to be happy you must have that person in your life in that way *all the time!* You might even catch yourself saying that you would "just die" without that person. Of course, you would not mean that. What you would mean is that it feels as though a big *part of you* would "die" if that person was not in your life.

Now here comes the fascinating thing about all this. In order *not* to have a big part of you die from being without that person, you will *kill* a big part of that person.

You will kill their spirit.

You will so smother them with your love, and with your need for *their* love, that they will choke, they will cough, and then they will have to throw you off in order to survive.

They will run away from you, which is sad, because they really liked you a lot, and probably could have loved you—but they simply could not fill your needs.

IT SOUNDS LIKE YOU'VE BEEN FOLLOWING ME AROUND.

I have! But that's not why I know this. I know this because this is the way love is being experienced by most of the human race. And that is because you have confused "love" with "need."

Now here is the good news. Remember this always: *You need nothing outside of yourself in order to be happy.*

I know that you think that you do, but you do not. This is an illusion. *It is the First of The Ten Illusions of Humans.*

The illusion is that need exists. The illusion is that someone or something outside of yourself is needed.

Yet if you still think that it is, try this exercise.

1. Make a list of the people, places, and things you think that you need to be happy.

2. Now think of a time when you did not have these, and were still perfectly happy.

3. Now ask yourself, "Why do I think I need this person, place, or thing to be happy now?"

If you are honest with yourself, you will know that you do not. You may *prefer* to create your happiness with this particular tool, but it is not necessary to do so.

Do not, therefore, turn a *preference* into a *need*.

? **EVERY TIME I GET A GIRLFRIEND, SHE GETS ME "OFF COURSE." I MEAN, THERE ARE CERTAIN THINGS THAT I WANT TO DO IN LIFE, BUT WHEN I GET HOOKED UP WITH A GIRL, I ALWAYS SEEM TO GO IN HER DIRECTION, OR IN SOME NEW DIRECTION SHE WANTS US TO TAKE TOGETHER, BUT I ABANDON MY OWN JOURNEY. WHAT'S ALL THAT ABOUT?**

—W., 19, Baton Rouge, Louisiana

It's about fear, my friend. It's about fear. You are afraid that your girlfriend of the moment will not stay in your life if you do as you had intended on doing with your career, or some other aspect of your life, and so you have given *up* your life in order to have the life that you *think* you want.

The difficulty with this is that, after a while, you become very clear that you are not living the life that you wanted, and you become surly, irritable, and moody. You can't say that anything in particular is "wrong," but nothing feels "quite right."

Soon, this feeling permeates your relationship, and, with luck, that relationship is over.

If you are not lucky the relationship will continue for a long time—and you will live a life of quiet desperation.

HOW CAN THAT CYCLE BE BROKEN?

Here are two important questions to ask in life.

1. Where am I going?

2. Who's going with me?

Most people ask themselves these questions at one time or another, but many of them make the mistake of putting the questions in reverse order. They ask the second question first.

Or, they may have them in good order when they first meet another, but then they change the questions around so they can get a better answer!

If you do either of these things, you may have great difficulty in relationships.

MY MOM AND I HAVE BEEN TRYING TO GET A FAMILY GOING—TO FIND A PARTNER FOR MY MOM AND A DAD FOR ME—BUT SO FAR IT HASN'T WORKED OUT. WHY?

—Jason, 14

Maybe it is not to be.

WHAT DOES THAT MEAN?

It means maybe there is perfection in things being just the way they are right now. All you have to do is see the perfection. That's all anyone has to do in any of the moments of their life in order to move from "unhappy" to "happy." Just see the perfection.

Whatever is happening, whatever is going on, see the perfection. Whatever is *not* happening that you wish would happen, see the perfection.

Then move into gratitude for it. Say an inner word of thanks.

HOW DO I DO THAT? HOW DO I SAY THANKS FOR A LIFE THAT IS NOT THE WAY I WANT IT?

By knowing that it *is* the way you want it at some level. By understanding that there is always a reason at the soul level why your life is the way it is, why things have happened the way they have happened, and why everything that is "showing up" is showing up.

WHAT'S THE REASON?

You are a spiritual being, and you came to the body to experience Who You Are. In order to do this you are, in every moment, drawing to you the exact and perfect people, places, and events to experience precisely what you came to your physical body to experience.

You are in the process of recreating yourself anew in every single moment of Now.

YOU'VE SAID THIS ALREADY.

I'm repeating it for emphasis. This is why you came here. This is what you are up to. Everything else is an illusion. This process is called evolution. It is the evolution of the soul.

Now, if you *know* this, everything changes. You no longer see things as you used to see them. You no longer experience tragedies as tragedies, but as opportunities. They are your chances to announce and to create, to be and to express, to become and to fulfill Who You Really Are.

The whole world has been created as a stage on which you may do that. Actually, the entire Universe is that stage, and your Earth is the part of it on which you stand.

? WHEN ARE YOU GOING TO SEND ME SOME-
ONE WHO WILL LOVE ME AND SEE ME FOR
EVERYTHING THAT I AM (MY QUIRKS, FLAWS, ETC.)
THE WAY I LOOK AT EVERYONE AND APPRECIATE
THEM?   —*Cary, 19*

I have sent you someone, Cary. Me!

WELL, YOU KNOW, GOD, I APPRECIATE THAT, BUT
WHAT I WOULD ALSO APPRECIATE IS ANOTHER
HUMAN BEING IN MY LIFE TO SHARE MY DAYS AND
NIGHTS WITH ME.

I know that. I understand that. Now I'm
going to tell you how to find that.

GREAT!

Simply be what you are looking for.

BE WHAT I AM LOOKING FOR?

Yes. Instead of searching for someone to
love, be someone who could be loved. Send
what you wish to receive. Be what you wish to
experience. This is the greatest secret in all of
life.

Be what you are looking for, and what you are looking for will find *you*.

Everyone is looking for the same thing. Do not, therefore, be the searcher. Rather, be that for which others are searching.

13

Drugs

WHAT IS EVERYONE SO SCARED ABOUT MY EXPERIMENTING A LITTLE WITH DRUGS?

—*Valerie, 17, Paris, France*

As we get started on this topic, let's get clear on our definitions. Drugs are drugs. It does not matter whether they are "legal" or "illegal." There are what some people call medicinal drugs and what some call recreational drugs. Abuse of either can create major problems. So can abuse of alcohol, which is a drug of a different sort.

Now the answer to your question is that experimenting "a little" with drugs is almost impossible for most human beings.

Drugs are powerful, Valerie, and they can take over your life before you even know what is happening. And that's the problem.

Most people swear—absolutely swear—that they can handle them. They get upset when other people say watch out, be careful, don't go near the stuff, because they think that they are bigger than that, larger than that, more able than other people to deal with that.

Many drivers feel the same way. A strange recklessness overtakes them when they get behind the wheel. They're better at negotiating the curves than the guy who went before them and didn't make it. Put the pedal to the floor. That's all they think about. Nothing's going to happen to me.

This point of view is also prevalent among many drinkers. The feeling is that you "can handle it," even though statistics show that the huge majority of others "crash" when taking this road. Statistics don't matter. Facts become irrelevant. The thrill of the experience is all that counts.

Add reckless driving to drugs or alcohol and you've got a lethal problem.

BUT FRIENDS THAT I KNOW *ARE* USING DRUGS, AND THEY THINK THEY ARE HANDLING THEM PRETTY WELL, WITHOUT ANY PROBLEMS.

The situation with drugs is that they distort your thinking. You think you can control yourself; you think that you *are* controlling yourself, but they control you. From the very first use. It's insidious.

Let me tell you the story of the lobster and the water.

One day a lobster was put in a cooking pot by a restaurant chef, and it never even tried to climb out. Do you know why? Because the water was cool. The lobster would have been clawing and clawing to get out if the water had been hot, but it was not.

Only after he got the lobster into the pot did the chef turn up the heat. And even then he put the water over a very low flame. It took a long time for the water to boil. By the time the water got hot enough to cook the lobster, the lobster did not even know what happened.

If you had asked the lobster in the first few minutes, "Why aren't you trying to climb out of there? Don't you see the trouble you are in?" the lobster would have replied, "Don't be silly. I'm just swimming around in the water here."

SO YOU THINK THAT MY FRIENDS ARE IN MORE TROUBLE THAN THEY KNOW.

Let's just say that they're in hot water.

I will say it again. Drugs start to control you from the very first use. You don't think so, but they do. The fact that you don't think so is *how* they do.

Drugs stop you from thinking the way you usually think. Take enough of them and they stop you from thinking at all.

"Oh, I'll know when to stop" are the famous last words of thousands of people who have had their lives ruined by drugs. The same can be said about alcohol.

MAYBE USING THIS STUFF *IS* DANGEROUS . . .

There is no "maybe" about it.[7]

. . . BUT THE PEOPLE I KNOW WHO DO IT ARE ONLY TRYING TO GET HIGH.

What's funny is that people do drugs, or drink alcohol, to experience getting "high," and they usually wind up very low. In fact, about as low as you can go.

And what's sad is they can get "high" without doing any of these things.

YEAH, YEAH, I KNOW. "GET HIGH ON LIFE."

Yea!

THAT JUST SEEMS SO—I DON'T KNOW—SAPPY.

Most of the world has made what is sensational, sappy, and what is sappy, sensational. In this, most of the world has it backward.

If it is a special sensation that you are looking for, there is nothing more sensational than life. Life as it really is, not life as it is experienced through the cloudy mist of a drugged mind, and a dragged-out body, and a desperate heart, and a dampened soul.

I am talking here about life as it is experienced through an enlightened mind and an energized body and an earnest heart and an elevated soul.

I am talking here about pure happiness, *real* happiness, not counterfeit happiness produced by artificial stimulants. I am talking about "being," "doing," and "having" at a very high level.

Being, Doing, and Having are the three levels of human experience. All experience springs from Being. Whatever you are Being will determine what you are Doing, and what you are Doing will determine what you are Having. You may not have thought about it that way, but that is the way it is.

Living happily is about being something, doing something, and having something that makes your soul dance and your heart sing and your mind blow.

HOW CAN I EXPERIENCE THAT? ARE YOU SAYING THAT I CAN EXPERIENCE THAT?

This whole book is saying that. That's what this whole book is saying. Everywhere you look on these pages you will find hints and clues and tools that you can use to be, do, and have what you choose.

Drugs will not give you that. Drugs are not among the tools. Drugs destroy the tools.

14

School

 WHY ARE WE TAUGHT FACTS, AND NOT IDEAS, IN SCHOOL? —*Tristan, 14*

Because ideas are dangerous, if one wants to keep things the way they are—and your society does.

Most societies are deeply invested in seeing things stay the way they are, because the way they are is what makes the society a "society."

A "society" is nothing more than a group of people formed around a particular way of seeing things. These people share traditions, mutually created institutions, activities, and interests. Anything that threatens those traditions, institutions, and interests must be opposed, and it certainly can't be *taught*.

Nothing is more threatening to all of this, of course, than new ideas. Children are, therefore, encouraged to "learn," but not to "think" too much.

Thinking involves the consideration of ideas. Learning involves simple memorization.

THAT'S *EXACTLY* WHAT IT INVOLVES. MEMORIZE THE PRESIDENTS! MEMORIZE THE CAPITALS! MEMORIZE THE BATTLES! HERE ARE THE FACTS. MEMORIZE THEM! THIS IS HOW IT IS, NOW JUST "GET THAT."

What makes this all the more challenging is that the facts are rarely really facts—that is, unvarnished statements of what is so, of what occurred. Too often they are particular *interpretations* of what is so and what occurred, designed to justify and solidify a particular point of view. It is this point of view that your elders seek to teach you, not simply bare facts.

Thus it is that children of the human race can have entirely different understandings of what happened, and why, when Japan placed its soldiers in Korea, or when the United States placed its soldiers in Vietnam, or when Israel placed its soldiers in the occupied territory of Palestine, depending upon whose children are listening to whose parents and reading whose accounts of "history."

In this way the sins of the fathers are visited upon the sons, even unto the seventh generation.

GREAT! SO I'M LOCKED INTO A SCHOOL SYSTEM THAT TEACHES ME HOW TO MAKE THE SAME MISTAKES THAT MY PARENTS MADE! TERRIFIC.

It doesn't have to be that way. You don't have to repeat those mistakes. Look around you and see which parts of how the world is you don't agree with. Then investigate the causes of things being that way, and decide to do something about them that could change things.

It could be said that there are essentially two kinds of people on your planet, The Repeaters and The Changers. The Repeaters are those who look at the past and repeat what was done then. The Changers are those who look at the past and change what is being done so as *not* to repeat it.

You can become one of The Changers.

AND ONE OF THE FIRST THINGS WE CAN CHANGE IS HOW SCHOOLS WORK!

That is one of the first things you would *have* to change if you wanted to change anything at all. For what you learn, you become. And it is very hard to "unbecome" that.

HOW CAN WE CHANGE SCHOOLS?

There may not be much you can do to change your school this year or next, or maybe not even in the near future, but you can change your *experience* of school.

Look at it a new way. See it, however imperfect, for what it is: a stepping-stone that life has put in place for you to get exactly where you choose to go.

Then use your new, more positive attitude to suggest some changes that you think could make the school better. Even in the least democratic schools there should be some mechanisms in place for doing this.

Have fun with it. Be a little daring. But try not be overly critical, or take yourself too seriously, or you will defeat yourself before you begin.

Pass on to your parents, to those in control at your school system, and, as you grow older, to anyone in your community who will listen, the best suggestions you have for changing your schools.

GOT ANY IDEAS?

You could try telling them to not emphasize "facts" in your schools, but rather, concepts. You could invite them to focus on the three Core Concepts of Holistic Living:

1. Awareness

2. Honesty

3. Responsibility

You could suggest they build their entire curriculum around these concepts. Do not abandon reading, writing, and arithmetic, nor any of the other "academics," but, rather, use them as tools with which to illustrate, and live, these concepts.

You could encourage them to create a program that includes many areas of human experience to explore, such as self-discovery and self-expression, sharing power, fairness economics, sustainable living, honoring diversity, utilizing differences, celebrating sexuality, creative thought, and the unity of all life.

Tell them that if they teach *these* subjects they won't have any problem keeping students in school—or holding their attention while they are there.

And while you are at it, tell them to try getting rid of grade levels that separate people by age, allowing students to fluidly group themselves by interests and passions.

And abolish tests, and scores, and marks, and measures, letting the joy in each child be the measure, and the sparkle in each eye and the excitement in each walk be the test, of whether brains are being stimulated or numbed.

And, lastly, why not suggest giving students a say in how their school is run, including them among the decision-makers in some real way, not in a "showcase" way?

 WHOA. WHAT A SCHOOL THAT WOULD BE![8]

AND ONE OF THE FIRST THINGS I WOULD CHANGE IS HOMEWORK. WHY DO WE HAVE TO HAVE THREE HOURS OF HOMEWORK AFTER SEVEN HOURS OF SCHOOL?   —*Wade, 15, Houston, Texas*

That is a question that even adults are looking at now. A recent study by the University of Michigan suggests that young children are seeing up to three times as much homework as children did twenty years ago.

If you feel that your homework load is way too heavy, speak to your parents about that, and ask them to talk with the school.

YOU THINK THAT'S GOING TO DO ANY GOOD? EVEN IF THEY DID TALK WITH THE SCHOOL, NOTHING WOULD HAPPEN.

You don't know that. That's what you *think*, but you don't *know that*.

The most debilitating thing you can do in life is to not try something because you think you already know how everything is going to turn out. This stops the energy from flowing even before it has a chance to start. Don't stop yourself before you start.

Remember that always: *Don't stop yourself before you start.*

When you stop yourself before you start, you are sure to get nowhere. Then you can make yourself right.

You knew all along that you were not going to get anywhere, and you didn't. You're not very happy, but at least you can say you're right.

This attitude is what allows people who are not very happy to stay unhappy. It is what allows people who are angry to stay angry. It is what allows people who are not getting anywhere to keep not getting anywhere.

Think positively. Throw negative thinking away. Positive thinking actually has a *physical effect* on life. It sends up vibes. It moves energy around in a particular way. *It creates positive outcomes.*

 I DON'T KNOW WHETHER TO HANG WITH THE POPULAR "PREPPY" KIDS OR THE CAST-

OFF "GRUNGY" KIDS. WHY DOES EVERYONE HAVE
TO SEPARATE LIKE THAT?

—*Mari, 16, Phoenix, Arizona*

Separating is a way of seeking identity. For
young people this feels particularly urgent. All of
life is a process of defining yourself, of deciding
who you are, and it is no different in school.

But remember what I said earlier, when the
discussion was about pressure in school. Don't
do anything that does not feel like "you" just to
be a member of a group.

Why not choose not to be "exclusive" with
one group or the other? Be yourself. If it feels as
though you'd like to spend some time with one
group, do it. If it feels as though you'd like to
spend time with the other, do it. Don't let either
group co-opt you.

Groups separate, individuals unite. It is the
job of groups to separate. That's what makes
them groups.

That's my "practical" answer. Would you like
to hear my spiritual answer?

SURE.

It is not necessary to separate from one
another in order to find one's identity, but it

sometimes seems that way to people who are living deeply within the illusion of disunity.

This illusion holds that unity is not the nature of things, but rather, disunity. According to this theory, everything is separate, with individual identities, purposes, and functions.

So, people believe that separation is necessary for them to be able to fully know themselves. In fact, exactly the opposite is true.

WHAT DO YOU MEAN?

I mean that it is in *unity*, not in disunity, that your true identity will be found. It is in oneness, not in separation, that your real self will be experienced.

EVERYTHING IS NOT SEPARATE? THINGS DO NOT HAVE INDIVIDUAL IDENTITIES, PURPOSES, AND FUNCTIONS?

If I told you that your purpose and function is the same as the tree outside your window, that it is the same as the mountain covered with snow, or the ocean lapping at the shore, would you believe me?

PROBABLY NOT.

Yet it is.

YOU'D HAVE TO EXPLAIN THAT TO ME.

The purpose and function of the tree is growth, and that is your purpose and function as well. It is the purpose and function of all of life.

You are growing into the grandest version of the greatest vision you ever held about Who You Are. So is the tree. The only difference is, you know it, and the tree does not. You know it at a conscious level, whereas the tree's level of consciousness is not the same as yours.

You are aware of your Self. That is, you are *self-conscious*. Compared to the tree, you are a more highly evolved being. But you are both "up to" the same thing.

I GOT IT WITH THE TREE. I DON'T GET IT WITH THE MOUNTAIN OR THE OCEAN.

You don't get that the mountain and the ocean are growing?

NO. IF ANYTHING, THEY ARE GETTING SMALLER.

Oh, I see. You equate "growth" with getting "bigger."

AND YOU DO NOT?

Growth is evolution in any form.

The mountain is changing all the time. So is the ocean. So is all of life. All change is growth. This is what evolution is about.

"Bigger" does not necessarily mean "better." Things can grow smaller, and be said to have greatly evolved.

I NEVER THOUGHT OF IT THAT WAY.

Well, that's the beauty of all really stimulating conversation. It invites you to think of things in new ways.

> **?** I HAVE THE WORST BIOLOGY TEACHER IN THE HISTORY OF THE WORLD! I AM FALLING *ASLEEP* IN THERE! WHAT AM I GOING TO DO? AND DON'T SAY, "CHANGE CLASSES," BECAUSE I'VE ALREADY TRIED THAT AND THERE AREN'T ANY OTHER OPTIONS. —*Dennis, 16, New York City*

217

Talk with the teacher. Tell the teacher that you just aren't "getting" it, and ask what you can do, maybe even outside of class, to help yourself.

Without making the teacher "wrong," tell the teacher that you are having a hard time keeping your interest up in class, and ask the teacher if there are any special projects, or methods, or experiments that you could use to stay more "into" what's being done.

Talk to some other students, and see if anyone is having an easier time of it than you. If you find a few (you probably will), ask the teacher if you could "team" with some of those students now and then on a project or assignment. (First ask the students if that would be all right.) This might not only be a way to enliven your experience of the class, it might also be a way for you to get to know some other kids a lot better.

Talk to your parents about it, and see if they have any suggestions. Go to your school counselor as well.

Whatever you do, don't just complain about it, but do nothing about it, and let that be the reason that you do not do well in class.

? **SOME OF THE KIDS ARE CHEATING IN CLASS, AND ON TESTS. THEY WANT ME TO JOIN THEM. I ACTUALLY COULD USE A LITTLE "ASSISTANCE" ON MY GEOMETRY TESTS, AND I SUPPOSE I COULD OFFER SOME TO A FEW OF MY FRIENDS WHO ARE NOT DOING WELL IN THE CLASSES THAT I LIKE—SOCIAL STUDIES AND FRENCH, FOR INSTANCE. BUT I KNOW THAT CHEATING IS WRONG, SO . . .** —*Marshall, 16, New Orleans*

There is no such thing as "right" and "wrong," as we discussed earlier. There is only what "works" and what "doesn't work," given what you are trying to do.

GREAT! WHAT I'M TRYING TO DO IS PASS GEOMETRY!

Is that all?

WHAT DO YOU MEAN, "IS THAT ALL"?

Is there nothing more you are trying to do?

UH, I DON'T THINK SO.

I think there is, although you may not be conscious of it.

219

SO WHAT IS IT YOU THINK THAT I AM TRYING TO DO?

You are deciding who you are. You are defining yourself. In every single moment, that is what every human being is doing.

YOU KEEP SAYING THAT.

The thing is, once you understand what you are *really* doing on this planet, rather than what it *looks like* you are doing when you buy into the illusion, everything changes.

The question changes.

The question is no longer, "Should I cheat on my exam?" or, "Can I get away with cheating?" the question becomes, "Is 'a cheater' who I really am? Am I a person who cannot be trusted? Is this who I want to be?"

HALF THE WORLD "CHEATS." MY DAD PROBABLY "CHEATS" ON HIS INCOME TAX.

And you can be like half of the world—a world, by the way, that you have more than once criticized for not being what you wanted it to be—or you can *be the change you would like to see in the world.*

15

Parents

 WHY CAN'T MY PARENTS STAY IN LOVE AND STAY MARRIED?

—Carrie, 15, San Francisco, California

Your parents *can* stay in love and stay married, but it would require a shift in the things they believe for them to do so.

Your parents would have to believe that love is a decision, not a reaction. Then they would have to decide to love each other in the way that they did when they first met.

In those days they forgave each other everything—if they even saw anything *to* forgive. This is because they imagined their self-interests to be identical. Now they imagine their self-interests to have diverged.

Sometimes people's interests *seem* to conflict, but it is rarely that they really do. This is because all people, ultimately, want the same thing.

All you have to do is identify the desire that's behind the desire that's behind the desire. You may have to dig deeply, sometimes, but at the core of someone else's desire you will almost always find your own—and an interest that you share in common.

It is in being willing to dig deeply to find this common interest that the work of love is done. It is in finding this common interest that its joy is made real.

Love says, "I know that you and I are one, and that we are both after the same thing, ultimately. There is something that we both desire here, and we simply think that there are different ways of achieving it.

"These different ways seem to conflict with each other right now, making it 'look like' we are in opposition—that we need to be 'opponents.' But I am willing to move out of opposition and into supposition.

"I am willing to suppose that somewhere, beneath all of this apparent conflict, we can find that desire that you and I share in common, and then co-create a way for us both to experience that."

In many, many instances such a shift in awareness can recreate a marriage anew.

Now, there are some instances when reaching this, achieving this understanding, leads to a return to love between people, but not a return to the old form of their relationship. For many very good reasons it may not work for them to do so. They decide that they will recreate their loving relationship in another way, which does not include remaining together.

You can be very okay and live a happy life if your parents do not stay together, but that would require a shift in the things *you* believe.

You would have to understand that you—and no other people, places, or things—are the source of your happiness, security, and love. You would have to believe that you are not the cause or in any way to blame for your parents' separation, that they still love you as much as they ever did, and that they will be there for you in the best way they can.

You would have to know that, even if they weren't able to be there for you, God is.

This means that you would have to trust life, to know that all things will work out for the highest good, that God is on your side, and that with the entire universe thus lined up with you, nothing can stop you from experiencing peace, happiness, love, and joy in your life, if you choose to.

This is the truth, I promise you. I will never leave you, and you can call on me at any time, in any moment, for strength, for courage, for insight, to catch your tears, and hold your heart, and quiet your mind, and heal your soul, and restore your whole Self to its magnificent wonder.

Believe in yourself, believe in me, believe in love—for these three are one, these three are eternal, these three will bless and grace the universe forever.

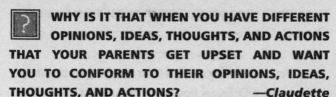

WHY IS IT THAT WHEN YOU HAVE DIFFERENT OPINIONS, IDEAS, THOUGHTS, AND ACTIONS THAT YOUR PARENTS GET UPSET AND WANT YOU TO CONFORM TO THEIR OPINIONS, IDEAS, THOUGHTS, AND ACTIONS? *—Claudette*

Parents naturally think that their opinions, ideas, thoughts, and actions are the ones that make sense, since they are the ones who had them and did them.

You think that your opinions, ideas, thoughts, and actions are the ones that make sense for exactly the same reason.

Human beings do not like *differences*, and the older they get, the less they like them. Humans like "sameness" because they assume that "sameness" validates their own "rightness."

In other words, if you are doing it the same as me, the way I'm doing it must be "right."

As soon as you do something different from me, I feel made wrong. Or, at least, I *can*, depending upon my level of inner security.

The human race has not been known to be particularly secure.

HOW CAN WE CHANGE THAT? WHEN I HAVE KIDS, I DON'T WANT TO BE MAKING THEM WRONG EVERY

**TIME THEY DO OR SUGGEST SOMETHING DIFFER-
ENT FROM ME.**

Inner security comes from moving back into
your own Original Power. It means understanding deeply the relationship between you and
God. It is about knowing that there is no such
thing as "right" and "wrong," there is only that
which works and does not work, depending
upon what it is you are trying to do.

The principles outlined in this book may help
you. Reviewing the conversations here may be
of assistance as you seek to create a place of
mind from which you can make this change in
you.

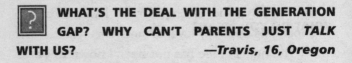

**WHAT'S THE DEAL WITH THE GENERATION
GAP? WHY CAN'T PARENTS JUST *TALK*
WITH US?** —*Travis, 16, Oregon*

Some parents do not feel "equipped" to talk
openly with their children. They feel that they
are speaking a different language. Coming from

a different place. Concerned about different things. Holding different values.

All of these things may, in fact, be true.

SO WHAT? SO WHY CAN'T THEY STILL TALK WITH US? DO WE HAVE TO AGREE ON EVERYTHING TO HAVE A MEANINGFUL CONVERSATION?

No. But often parents feel the same way that teenagers say that teenagers do. Unheard. Misunderstood. Disappeared.

PARENTS **FEEL THIS WAY? HOW CAN THEY FEEL THIS WAY WHEN THEY ARE THE ONES WHO ARE NOT HEARING—MISUNDERSTANDING AND DISAPPEARING US?**

Everything that you experience in yourself you will see across the room, if you look closely enough.

WHAT DO YOU MEAN?

I mean that the whole world is a mirror, reflecting yourself back to you. If you feel unheard, misunderstood, and disappeared, it may be because *that is how you make others feel.*

227

Put another way, if you make others feel completely heard, deeply understood, and totally present during a moment when they are with you, it will be very, very difficult (probably impossible) for *you* to feel unheard, misunderstood, or disappeared in that same moment.

What goes around, comes around.

Once you know that your parents can feel the same way you do, the door of opportunity swings open. You have a chance to establish some real communication.

I WONDER. SOMETIMES I WONDER IF I'LL EVER HAVE A MEANINGFUL TALK WITH MY PARENTS AGAIN. THEY SEEM SO DISTANT.

Well, this is what we have been talking about, isn't it? Some parents feel that their teenage sons and daughters are "distant." So the feeling is mutual.

OKAY THEN, WHY? WHY IS THIS HAPPENING?

The separate generations think that they have different interests and different goals. Actually, all human beings have the same goals and are interested in the same thing: being themselves, and experiencing that at the next highest level, and the next, and the next.

The scientific name for this process is *evolution*, and it is what is going on everywhere.

Very few people on *either* side of what you call the "generation gap" see this, however. They imagine that they each want something different—and they also imagine that it is the other generation that is standing in their way of getting it.

And, you are right. This is because the two generations do not talk to each other, because they think they have nothing in common. So the circle completes itself and there *is* a "generation gap."

SO? WHAT DO WE DO?

Change it. Be one of The Changers.

There are a lot of ways you can get this process going.

You can have discussions with older adults—even create regular discussion nights and form discussion circles—at your local youth center, at the senior citizens' center, or at the community center (neutral turf!) in your town.

You can ask each other questions on all manner of things, get each other's opinion, and even give each other advice.

You can also just start talking to your parents. And if they won't listen, write to them. Most will read what you have to say. And in the written stuff, ask them again to sit down with you and listen to you. But you must also be willing—and tell them you are—to listen to them.

Tell them these could be some of the last chances that you will ever have to just sit down and talk together, to look at life, to share feelings, and thoughts, and ideas together. Tell them it's important to you.

Make the first move. Take the first step. As I said, many of your parents think that you don't *want* to talk with them. They think you're bored with their ideas, and don't want to hear from them. They think that you just want them to leave you alone. So they do.

It's the easy way out. Don't let them take it. And don't YOU take it. You want to close the generation gap? Close it. Do it. It's up to you. Most parents, most adults, will come halfway if you do. Okay, not all of them. There are those who won't. But most of them will.

Give it a try. You might surprise yourself.

WHY IS IT THAT MY PARENTS NOTICE ONLY THE THINGS THAT I DO WRONG?

—Bryan, 16, Omaha, Nebraska

Most parents do not notice only the things you do wrong. Most parents also notice the things you do right. *They just don't say anything about it.*

People in general do not dwell on the positive, but, instead, emphasize the negative. This is a habit of most human beings. (It might even be one of yours.)

If people understood "the power of positive thinking," they would never dwell on the negative again.[9]

SO, HOW CAN I GET MY PARENTS TO *SAY* SOMETHING WHEN THEY *SEE* SOMETHING THAT I AM DOING RIGHT?

By saying something when *you* see something that *they* are doing right.

Remember this always: *What goes around, comes around.*

If you told your parents every time you saw them doing something that you thought was good, or cool, or helpful, or of benefit to you, you would probably shock them out of their

231

minds. You would also open the door to receiving such energies in return.

You could even make that a neat bumper sticker:

> **SAY SOMETHING GOOD
> WHEN YOU SEE SOMETHING RIGHT.**

That little slogan, *implemented*, could change the world.

WHY DO I ALWAYS HAVE TO BE THE ONE TO START? WHY CAN'T *THEY* DO IT WITHOUT MY HAVING TO SHOW THEM HOW?

That's a fair question, and it gives me a chance to get across another very valuable piece of information. So, thanks for asking it.

Remember this always: *What you seek from another, give to another. That which you wish to experience, cause another to experience.*

YOU MEAN I HAVE TO GIVE SOMETHING IN ORDER TO GET IT?

No, you don't have to. It's just the fastest way. It's the way to use the Power of Creation at its optimum level.

I DON'T GET IT. HOW AM I CREATING SOMETHING IN MY LIFE IF I AM GIVING IT AWAY?

First of all, what goes around, comes around, as I've just said. So what you give to others comes back to you, usually multiplied.

SO *THAT'S* WHY YOU SAY, "DO UNTO OTHERS AS YOU WOULD HAVE IT DONE UNTO YOU"!

Yes! That is more than just a nice saying. That is *what actually happens*.

What you do unto others *will be* done unto you, sooner or later. This is the Law of Ultimate Return. It has nothing to do with punishments or rewards. It's simply how things are. It's how everything works. Life is a boomerang, and what you send out, you get back. *It is inevitable.*

So here is the best advice I could ever offer you as you move through your teen years and become adults:

What you seek from another, give to another. What you seek from the world, give to the world. What you seek from life, give to life.

If you want great vibes coming in, send great vibes out!

Be the source of that which you wish to receive.

BUT DOESN'T THIS CONTRADICT WHAT YOU SAID EARLIER ABOUT NEVER DOING ANYTHING TO PLEASE ANOTHER?

No. What I went on to say was, do what you do for another not to please *them,* but because it pleases *you.* And I also said that, in order to notice *how* it pleases you, you must look closely at where you and the other share a common interest.

When you recognize this common interest, then you are able to see that what you are doing "for" someone else is really being done for you.

This includes doing unto others as you would have it done unto you. It *especially* includes that.

BUT HOW CAN I GIVE AWAY SOMETHING THAT I DON'T HAVE? IF I NEED MORE MONEY IN MY LIFE, HOW IN THE WORLD CAN I GET IT BY GIVING IT AWAY?

The idea that you don't have enough of something is an illusion. That is, it may *look like* you don't have enough, but in Ultimate Reality

you do. In order to experience this, find someone who has less of whatever it is that you
desire. Now give that person some of what little you imagine yourself to have. You will immediately experience that *you have had enough of it
all along. So much, in fact, that you can actually
give it away.*

In that moment you will change your life.

You will shift your reality.

This shift from "not enough" to "enough,"
from "insufficiency" to "sufficiency," will change
the way you hold your experience of yourself—
and thus, the way you produce it. Because . . .
what you THINK, you CREATE.

So now, to get back to your original question, the question that started all of this . . . if
you feel that you are not experiencing enough
of the good feelings that come from having the
things you are doing right noticed by your parents, cause your parents to experience enough
of the good feelings that come from having the
things *they are doing right* noticed by *you.*

Now the magic will happen. First, *you will
feel good immediately,* simply noticing how good
they feel when you do this. Second, you will
invoke the Law of Ultimate Return, and you will
be noticed for the things that you are doing
well.

235

> ❓ **I KEEP HEARING THAT AS YOU SOW, SO SHALL YOU REAP. BUT THAT'S NOT ALWAYS TRUE. I TREAT A LOT OF PEOPLE IN A CERTAIN WAY WHO DO NOT TREAT ME THAT WAY.**
>
> **—Tomas, 18, Cape Town, South Africa**

I agree that this is sometimes the case. You cannot always depend on receiving from a person the same thing that you give to that person.

OKAAAAY, SO NOW I'M TOTALLY CONFUSED. I THOUGHT YOU SAID, "WHAT GOES AROUND, COMES AROUND."

I did, but I did not say from *where*.

What you put into life will come back from life—but not necessarily from the same place into which you put it. Sometimes it will come from the same place, but by no means always. Yet what *will* happen is that it will come back from *somewhere*. Sooner or later this will occur. If you pay close enough attention to life and how it is, you will see this law working.

BUT WHY CAN'T IT COME BACK FROM THE PERSON I *GIVE* IT TO? LIKE LOVE. WHY CAN'T THE PEOPLE I LOVE, LOVE ME?

The Law doesn't work that way. It would be too easy to manipulate everyone with it if it did. Besides, you really don't want people to love you because you love them. Trust me. You want people to love you not as a *return* for what you give *them,* but as an honest response and reaction to how you are in the world—whether you do something specifically for them or not.

Do not, therefore, fall into the trap of treating someone nicely just so that they will treat *you* nicely. If you're not careful, that could develop into a manipulation. Treat others nicely simply because *that's who you are,* and that's who you *choose to BE*.

It is from this place of "beingness" (yup, here we go again) that you create your reality. Always and forever, this is true.

WHY DO PARENTS ALWAYS HAVE TO ACT LIKE "PARENTS"? WHY CAN'T THEY LET THEIR HAIR DOWN A LITTLE? LAST NIGHT I FOUND MY DAD AND MOM "MAKING OUT," AND YOU WOULD HAVE THOUGHT I CAUGHT THEM ROBBING A BANK OR SOMETHING. *—Tammy, 13*

Parents sometimes feel that they have to portray a certain image to their children—and being romantic or sexual in front of them is often not part of that. Unless it is. It depends upon what your parents, themselves, think about these things, and what they would like you to think about them.

If they want you to enjoy these things, they will let you see *them* enjoy them. If they want you to feel comfortable with these experiences, they will let you see *them* being comfortable with them.

Parents who act like "parents" do so because that is what they think that they are "supposed to do" in front of their children.

Children are rarely fooled by this, however. They see that their parents are wearing The Emperor's New Clothes.

WHAT DOES THAT MEAN?

Ask your parents!

? **WHEN I BECOME A PARENT WILL I MAKE THE SAME MISTAKES THAT TODAY'S PARENTS ARE MAKING? WILL I DO THE SAME THINGS THAT THEY ARE DOING NOW, EVEN THOUGH I HATE SOME OF WHAT THEY ARE DOING? THE REASON THAT I ASK YOU THIS IS THAT MY PARENTS SAY THAT I WILL. THEY KEEP SAYING, "WHEN YOU HAVE CHILDREN OF YOUR OWN, YOU'LL SEE THINGS DIF-FERENTLY." WILL I? I HOPE NOT.**

—Sandra, 15, Knoxville, Tennessee

You will see things differently, there is no doubt. Every *day* you see things differently. That is called growth. That is called change. That is called evolution. That is something you *want* to have happen. But that does not mean that you will do things the same way as your parents.

You may, or you may not. You will, unless you don't. What will cause you to do one thing or the other is your idea about yourself. Every moment you are defining yourself. Every day you are deciding who you are, and who you wish to be.

Most people do not see life in this way. Most people do not consider themselves to be actively engaging in this process. The turning point in life comes when you do.

You can begin to decide now what it means to you to be the thing called "parent." Do you choose to have a genuine friendship with your children? Do you choose for them to be able to come to you with any problem, to ask any favor, to seek any advice?

Everything your parents gave you was a gift. Not just the things you want to emulate, but the things you want to eliminate. Not just the things you want to remember, but the things you want to forget. Not just the things that made you laugh, but the things that made you cry.

All of it was a treasure. All of it. For it is from the lot of it that you will pick and choose, it is from the whole of it that you will select, it is from the all of it that you will come to know the part of it that you wish to call You.

This is not only true of what you received from your parents, but from all of life.

16

The Future

 WILL I THRIVE IN THE FUTURE WHEN I GROW UP? WILL I BE STRUGGLING?
—*Walter, 14, Ashland, Oregon*

 CAN YOU GIVE ME A GLIMPSE OF WHAT MY FUTURE HOLDS?
—*Jeanne, 15*

Jeanne, Walter, I am not creating your future, you are.

People keep asking me, God, what's going to be in my future? And I keep saying, "I don't know. What *is* going to be in your future?" And they say, but you're supposed to know! And I say, "But you're supposed to know." And they say, but you have the power to decide! And I say, "But you have the power to decide!"

You see, here is how life works. You decide what you choose, and then I make it happen. It is not the other way around.

The problem is, you think it is the other way around. You think that I decide what I choose, and it is up to you to make it happen. This reversal of the whole God-human relationship is what has created the twisted and distorted experience that you are having on your planet.

SO YOU'RE SAYING THAT I CAN HAVE WHATEVER I WANT?

No. God says, you cannot have what you want.

WHAT?

I said, you cannot have what you want. And the more you want something, the less chance there'll be that you'll *ever* have it.

WHAT ARE YOU TALKING ABOUT?

This is the Process of Creation.

Remember what I said about how you create your reality? You do so with thoughts, words, and deeds. Now if you are thinking "I want a partner for my mom and a dad for me," what you *will* have is the experience of "wanting one."

WHY? WHAT ARE YOU TALKING ABOUT?

I am saying that as you speak it, so will it be done unto you. In the beginning was the Word, and the Word was made flesh.

MAN, YOU'VE LOST ME.

What you THINK is what you create. What you SAY is what you CREATE. What you DO is what you create.

If you THINK you "want" so-and-so, if you SAY you "want" so-and-so, and if you ACT AS

IF you "want" so-and-so, then you will absolutely create the experience of WANTING IT.

Try to remember that the words "I" and "I AM" are the keys that turn the ignition in the engine of creation. Whatever comes after the word "I" or "I AM" will come to you in your experience.

If you say "I WANT something . . . " that will be your experience. You will have the experience of *wanting it*.

Therefore, guard your thoughts, words, and actions, and make sure that they reflect what you choose to experience in your life.

YOU MEAN I HAVE TO WATCH EVERY WORD THAT I SAY?

No. That would make everyone crazy. But you would do well to take stock of how you *usually* think, and the things you *frequently* say, and the way you *often* act.

Continually thinking, talking, and acting in a certain way produces enormous vibes, as we've discussed before. These energy vibrations are what create your reality.[10]

? **IS THE EARTH GOING TO TILT ON ITS AXIS, OR FALL INTO THE SEA, THANKS TO A GIANT QUAKE OR SOMETHING? EVERYONE KEEPS TALKING ABOUT STUFF LIKE THAT.**

—*Gina, 14, San Diego, California*

Stop talking about it, Gina. Start talking about how wonderful it's going to be on the Earth in the future. Then, if you wish, choose to do something about it.

I have no plans for the ultimate destruction of the planet. Do you?

Encourage your elders to take care of the environment. Ask them to monitor your world's global temperature and take measures to keep it within the range that has made it a paradise. Beg them to stop putting elements into the upper atmosphere that create holes in the protective layer that was placed over the Earth.

Ask older adults to stop depending upon fossil fuels and further polluting your atmosphere. They do not have to do this. There are ways to produce energy without doing this.

Urge them to preserve the forests, and stop cutting them down so that they can have their Sunday newspaper. You can grow a small plant in the ground that will provide you with all the paper you want or need.

You can also build houses out of something other than lumber. The present older generation is devastating your planet's own oxygen creation-and-purification system for no reason at all.

Ask the present older generation to keep your water pure. And stop using so much of it. Give the Earth a chance to replenish itself. Incredible stress is being placed on your natural systems. It is not required that this be so.

Your nutrient-rich topsoil is almost all gone. Corporate farming groups refuse to rotate crops or give growing fields a chance to reconsitute themselves. So, they put chemicals into the soil to try to do the job of nature. Humans are chemicalizing themselves to death.

SO "DOOMSDAY" IS RIGHT AROUND THE CORNER, IS THAT WHAT YOU ARE SAYING?

No. Not unless you decide that it is. Your species is making that decision right now, through the thousand and one choices being made every day.

The good news: the older you get, the more you have a voice in those choices. In short, your voice is the voice that can change the world.

**YOU KEEP TALKING ABOUT "CHANGING THE WORLD."
I'M TIRED ALREADY AND I HAVEN'T EVEN STARTED!
ISN'T THERE ANY TIME FOR ME JUST TO RELAX?
CAN'T WE JUST HANG OUT FOR A WHILE BEFORE
TACKLING EVERYTHING THAT'S GOING WRONG?**

Great question! And the answer is yes! Not only can you hang out *before* tackling the problems and challenges of the world, you can relax *while* you're doing it!

Relaxation is a huge and important part of the mix, and I'm glad you brought it up. You don't have to walk into Tomorrow with the weight of the world on your shoulders. In fact, it will do no one any good if you do that.

Have fun with life!

Have fun. Spread joy. Share love.

That is the Three-Way Path.

Have fun. Spread joy. Share love.

That is the Triune Mission.

Have fun. Spread joy. Share love.

That is the Triple Crown of the Human Race.

17

Suffering and Death

**WHY MUST MANY PEOPLE SUFFER IF YOU HAVE
THE POWER TO MAKE EVERYONE HAPPY?**

—*Eric, 13*

My wonderful Eric, this is a question that has
been asked since the beginning of time. And the
reason people keep asking it is that the answers
they have been given do not make sense.

The human race has been told, Eric, that suffering is good. Some teachers have even said that I *require* you to suffer, or that suffering helps you "pay for your sins," or that you can "offer it up" for the "poor souls in purgatory," meaning that I will release your ancestors from their torment sooner if you are in torment longer.

This last teaching is particularly sad. It paints a picture of me as some insane, insidious, insatiable God who would encourage your anguish as a bribe to grant an "early parole" to your loved ones; who would say, "You can end *their* suffering by beginning *yours*—but *someone is going to have to suffer here.*"

The whole idea is so opposite to who and what you imagine a loving, caring God to be, and yet it has been taught for centuries by one of your world's most powerful religions.

These and other beliefs have caused people to endure terrible agonies, and for no reason. I do not wish people to suffer. The reason that I do not stop human beings from doing whatever they are doing is that I have given human beings free choice to create and experience their lives as they choose. If I took away this free choice and just told them how things are "going to be

249

from now on," the entire purpose of life itself would be thwarted.

That purpose has now been stated many times. It is to provide each human soul with the opportunity to experience itself fully, freely creating the conditions that will allow it to do so.

Now, just for the record here, I never said that suffering is good, and I certainly never suggested that you should require yourself to suffer more than you would require your own animals to suffer in the face of unrelenting pain.

LAST SUMMER WE PUT OUR VERY SICK CAT TO SLEEP BECAUSE THE VET SAID SHE WAS SUFFERING SO MUCH AND THAT IT WAS ONLY THE HUMANE THING TO DO. HOW COME YOU LET US DO THIS FOR ANIMALS, BUT SEND US TO HELL IF WE DO IT FOR HUMANS?

—Marsha, 13, Birmingham, Alabama

I do not send you to hell, Marsha, for this or any other reason. You have pointed out a contradiction that reveals the confusion of the human race around the experience of suffering.

Of course, it makes no sense at all to treat a

cat more humanely than your grandmother. Logic tells you that no living creature should have to suffer pointlessly.

DOES THAT MEAN THAT HELPING SOMEONE DIE BECAUSE THEY ARE SO SICK IS OKAY?

Doctors do it all the time. They just don't tell anyone about it. Families have quietly asked for this, and in some cases have done it themselves. So, clearly, there are some circumstances in which human beings have felt that it is okay. But you must be aware that the civil laws in most places prohibit it. So, you could go to jail if you do it.

 WHY DO WE MAKE SUCH DUMB LAWS?
 —Enrique, 15, Mexico City

Neither human laws nor human theologies have ever been required to make sense.

Working to change laws that make no sense is one thing that young people could do to make a real difference in the world.

> **?** BUT IF YOU ARE SO POWERFUL, WHY DON'T
> YOU JUST END SUFFERING FOREVER? WHY
> NOT JUST ELIMINATE IT AS A POSSIBLE HUMAN
> EXPERIENCE? —*Brad, 15*

I have given you the tools with which to do that, Brad. But human beings have free will, and so far you have not chosen to use these tools.

Most of the conditions on your planet that cause people to suffer have been created by humans, and these conditions humans can just as easily "uncreate." They simply refuse to do so.

A huge percentage of human diseases—nearly all of them, actually—are preventable simply by changing human behaviors.

All of the deaths caused by human disagreement and war are also preventable simply by changing human behaviors, which can be done by changing human beliefs.

Even most accidents are preventable by changing human beliefs and behaviors.

Emotional distress, worry, fear, guilt, depression, and mental anguish are just as preventable, again by just changing human behaviors.

CAN YOU GIVE ME SOME EXAMPLES?

People could stop smoking, for example, and avoid millions of hours of suffering and thousands of deaths every year.

People could stop eating the flesh of dead animals and do the same thing.

People could stop making guns easily obtainable, and drugs available on every street corner, and do the same.

People could stop dumping chemicals into rivers and streams, releasing poisons into the air, cutting down millions of trees—much of them irreplaceable old growth—and stop depleting the other resources of the Earth faster than the Earth can replenish them.

People could decide—simply *decide*—that no matter what their individual, national, or international disagreements, they are not going to kill each other over them, but will find some other way to work things out.

People could decide to discontinue living with secrets and lies and hypocrisy, and just start telling the truth to each other.

People could create a new bottom line in their lives, changing their priorities, broadening their definition of Self, and deepening their understanding of love.

They could do all of these things, and more.

WHY DON'T THEY? WHY IN THE WORLD DON'T THEY?

Short-term gain. They do not want to give up their short-term gain. Whether it's short-term pleasure or short-term profit, they are not willing to give it up. In this they are very short-*sighted*, unable to see or acknowledge the long-term damage they are doing to themselves and to others.

MAN, THIS DOESN'T MAKE THINGS SEEM VERY HOPEFUL TO ME. YOU SAID THIS BOOK CAME TO ME TO TELL ME THAT THE HOPELESSNESS HAS ENDED. I DON'T GET IT.

The conditions and circumstances that cause suffering in the world are reversible. All that your society has to do is change beliefs, and then its behaviors. That is where the hope comes in.

You are "the society" of tomorrow. And with the tools you have been given here, you can produce a newer world, should you choose.[11]

The chief behavior humans are now being invited to change is the tendency to seek short-term gratification, and to be blind to long-term consequences.

If you see some of this behavior in yourself, you can start the process of changing that now, if you wish. You don't even have to wait until you are older. You can create some new behaviors right now, so that in a few short months when you are ready to move onto the larger stage of life, you will be prepared for your role.

WHAT CAN I DO NOW?

See if it makes you happy to look a little further down the road when you are making choices and decisions. Ask yourself what you'd like to experience in the long run, and what serves that intention.

For instance, if you think it will make you happy to get through school without a lot of frustration, hassle, and worry, does it serve you to put off that assignment or skip that class right now because you want to do something else?

If you think it will make you happy to go through life without a lot of health complications or emotional challenges and difficulties, does it serve you to use that drug or abuse your body with alcohol because right now you think it might feel good?

This is your life you are creating here, and you can do whatever you wish. Yet know that you are not creating only this second, this minute, this hour. You are creating parts of the rest of your life, right here, right now, in these days and times.

Remember this always: *Choices and decisions made in the moment are rarely limited in their impact to the moment in which they are made.*

Put another way: Very often you are deciding more than you think you are deciding.

Now this doesn't mean that you should turn yourself into an overcautious mouse. It does mean that you are invited to consider carefully all of the potential outcomes of the choices you are making—including the outcomes that could occur a little farther into the future.

This is something that today's older adults have not always done. In fact, they have rarely done it. Yet do not be too hard on them. Most of the human race has been living in an illusion.

Only recently has information about the true nature of life, and everyone's role in it, been available in clear, easily understandable terms.

WHEN WILL HUMAN SUFFERING COME TO AN END? —*Wesley, 16*

When humans change their behaviors, Wesley. And when they understand that the experience of suffering itself is an experience they are creating.

Right now, suffering from all conditions—all of them—can be healed.

IT CAN?

Yes. Not all of the conditions can be cured, but all can be healed.

THERE'S A DIFFERENCE?

Yes. A cure is a change in the condition, a healing is a change in the way a condition is experienced.

For instance, you can have a condition called "a headache" and you can change the way it is experienced without changing the fact that you are in that condition.

You have all done this. You have simply decided that having a headache is not going to interfere with something you want to do, and you go ahead and do it anyway, headache or not. Soon, you experience yourself having a headache, but not suffering from it.

This is what is meant by "healing" without "curing."

Often, such healing *produces* a cure. Spontaneously, the headache goes away.

I use this as a simple example, because it is very common. Human beings have used this process on conditions much more serious than a headache. Such healings are called blessings, and such cures are often called miracles.

Pain and suffering are not the same thing. Pain is a physical or emotional experience, and suffering is your point of view about it.

I DON'T UNDERSTAND. WHAT'S THAT SUPPOSED TO MEAN?

It means that one can have pain without having suffering. Pain is something you feel, suffering is a label you can put on it.

WHO DO YOU KNOW WHO HAS PAIN WHO IS NOT SUFFERING? AM I CRAZY HERE?

You are not crazy and it is a good question. But there is also a good answer.

Plenty of people have pain without experiencing suffering. Mothers giving birth are one example. Many mothers who give birth not only do not suffer during the process, they actually *welcome* whatever pain may come, and rejoice in it.

Many people with chronic pain (pain that continues day after day) resulting from some injury or illness have learned to live with it without suffering. Some are so happy to be alive that they have moved to a level of mastery over pain that others would consider intolerable.

There are other instances, as well, where physical pain has not necessarily produced suffering. Having a tooth pulled might be painful, but could be a *relief* from suffering. This is but one example, and there are many others.

As for emotional pain, a growing number of humans are experiencing that it can be a path to healing, and so, need not be a source of suffering, but of growth. Grief is one example. Anger that is allowed to be expressed safely and appropriately, without danger to self or others, is another.

So, pain and suffering are not the same thing. If you want suffering to end when pain is present, change your mind about the purpose for which it is present. *Use* your pain. Think of it as a tool in the fashioning of your experience.

? I HAVE LOTS OF QUESTIONS. I KNOW YOU SAID IF I HAD ONE QUESTION I COULD ASK OF GOD, WHAT WOULD IT BE, BUT I HAVE LOTS OF THEM. HERE ARE A FEW. WHY DO PEOPLE DIE? ARE WE LIVING IN HELL? IS MY LIFE SOMEONE'S DREAM? WHAT IS HEAVEN LIKE? WHY CAN'T PEOPLE LIVE FOREVER? —*Andrea, 17*

Ha! Thanks, Andrea! Thanks for just "going for it"! Let's take your questions one at a time.

People do not die, Andrea, they just change form. For a time they exist in the form that you call "human beings." Then they take the form that you have called "spirit beings." They may turn to human form whenever they wish, and they may take other forms as well.

You are all Divine Beings, eternally taking some form or another. You are Gods in formation. Or, to put this another way, *you are God's information.*

Yet why do you do this? Why do people do the thing that you *call* "die"? Because all of life is a cycle, and human beings go through their cycles just like everything else.

Even if you didn't think you had to (and, by the way, you never did have to), you would eventually choose to leave your present body and return to spirit, because it is the nature of life itself to unite with All That Is (what you call God), and then to emerge from that Allness as an individual version of it, and then to return to the Allness once again, and to repeat this cycle over and over again through all eternity.

YOU MEAN THERE'S NO END TO IT? I NEVER GET TO "STAY WITH GOD FOREVER"?

You do not want there to be an "end to it," because if there was, life itself would end. For this cycle IS life. Life is the breathing in and breathing out of God.

Even as the moon revolves around the Earth and the Earth revolves around the sun, so does everything in life revolve in and out of unity with the Allness.

WHY?

You cannot experience being anything unless its opposite exists. You cannot know yourself as "tall" unless "short" exists, or experience yourself as "warm" unless "cold" exists. You see?

If you never experienced yourself as "cold," you would not know what it was to be warm. In fact, if it were always the same temperature, every hour, every day, all the time, you would not even know what temperature it was. In the absence of some other temperature, the experience of temperature itself would disappear.

Similarly, in the absence of something other than God, the experience of God itself would disappear. If you were always experiencing being united with All That Is, you would never experience being REunited with All That Is, because you would never be away from All That Is.

Because your soul, which is a part of God, intuitively knows this, it will continually cycle in and cycle out of the experience of unification with All That Is.

It will become One With Everything, and then birth itself as an individual Part of Everything, connected to All Of It, but separate from it, even as your hand is connected to your toe as part of the same body, but separate from it.

This is what is meant by being born again. And you will be born again many times.

You are not living in hell. Hell does not exist. Yet you can create the illusion of hell, and you "sure as hell" will experience it.

Hell is the experience of forgetting who you really are. It is thinking that you are separate from me, forever. Hell is thinking that you are unworthy, unloved, and unlovable. Hell is thinking that you are useless, hopeless, and pointless. You are none of these things, but hell is not remembering who you really are.

There is one sure way of all of you remembering who you are. Remind others of who *they* are. If each of you will remind each other, all of you will remember.

That is part of the work you could be doing while you are on Earth, if you choose. It is wonderful work. It is fun, it is joyful, and it is loving.

HOW CAN I DO THIS? HOW CAN I REMIND THEM OF "WHO THEY REALLY ARE"?

It's so simple that it's shocking. You can do it with a smile. With a kind word. And with any expression of love.

263

With these small gestures (which can be really big gifts) you can give people back to themselves. You can return them to their grandest idea of who they are. You can return them to their power. To their Original Power.

You asked what heaven is like. This comes as close as anything to describing it. Heaven as a place does not exist. Heaven is a state of mind. It is the experience of our Oneness with All That Is, and the awareness that we *are that* even when we are not experiencing it.

You also asked if you are living someone's dream. That is a very interesting question, and the answer is yes. You are living yours.

The life you are living is a dream. An illusion. When you do the thing that you call "die" what you actually do is "wake up" from this dream. You step out of the illusion, and into Ultimate Reality—which you call Heaven. This Ultimate Reality is a place of consciousness, not a physical location.

Now to answer your final question . . . people DO "live forever." Life is eternal, and "death" is only a horizon. In the moment of your death, you will know this.

**? WHY AND HOW DO YOU CHOOSE WHEN
SOMEONE IS TO DIE? MY FATHER DIED VERY
SUDDENLY WHEN I WAS SMALLER, AND I'VE
NEVER UNDERSTOOD WHY.   —Victoria, 14**

God does not choose when people die, Victoria. I did not decide that your father should
die when you were so young. Your father died
when he did because it was the next step in the
journey of his soul.

Everything is perfect in God's world, and the
soul is always receiving the experience that it is
perfect for it to receive.

I know that this has been the saddest thing in
your life, and talking about perfection will not
take the sadness away. Nor should it.

It is very okay to be sad. You do not have to
apologize for that, or try to "fix it." There is a
way, though, that you may be able to use it.

You may be able to turn your sadness into a
tool that helps you, and others, during your life.
In this way you can give it purpose.

Enormous sadness about something like the
loss you've experienced can transform people
into compassionate, sensitive, and deeply caring
human beings. Where once they might have
been tempted to start down the road to being
sullen and angry for the rest of their lives, they

can make a choice to turn instead toward happiness and love.

Those who do are uniquely prepared and perfectly equipped to help others who have faced huge sadness in their lives, and may find great satisfaction and joy in doing so.

IS THAT WHAT I'M SUPPOSED TO DO?

There are no "supposed to's" in life. There is no blueprint that you must follow, no "mission" upon which you must embark. There is only choice. Pure choice. All the time, every day.

Each moment you are invited to ask yourself, "How can I use what I have been given by life?" When your answer is a positive one, you reaffirm the purpose of life itself, which is to recreate yourself anew in the next grandest version of the greatest vision you ever had about who you are.

You can make this up as you go along. You do not have to decide this for a lifetime right here, right now, in this moment. But each moment you can *ask the question*, and find the answer that works and that makes sense and that brings you happiness, peace, and joy right now.

Already you may have noticed that many of your friends turn to you when they need someone to talk to, when they want someone to listen, and maybe even give a little advice.

This does not happen by accident. You have already begun to vibrate with the energy of deep understanding and compassion for others who are experiencing confusion, pain, and hurt. What you do with that part of who you are is your decision. But there is no question that it is there—and it is there *because of your own life experiences*.

And so, in some way that you may now be able to more fully understand, your father's death so early in your life was also the next step in the journey of YOUR soul.

Like two threads in an enormous tapestry, your dad's life and yours have been woven together, intertwined in a beautiful design.

I JUST WISH THAT SOMEONE COULD TELL ME WHAT THE PICTURE IS SUPPOSED TO LOOK LIKE, SO THAT I COULD AT LEAST UNDERSTAND WHY THINGS HAD TO HAPPEN THE WAY THEY DID.

My wonderful friend, the reason that no one can tell you this is that the tapestry is not yet finished. *You are creating the picture right now.*

As is your father.

Do you think that he has died? I tell you that

he has not died, and can never die. He lives forever, and even forever more, and this is *not the last time that your paths will cross.*

Nor was it the first.

No soul joins the body, or leaves it, at a time that is inappropriate or wrong or "too early" or "too late."

The full agenda of the soul is not always known at the conscious level of the mind—nor can it be known or understood in the minds of others. Yet I can assure you that it makes perfect sense to your father now. And the day will come when it will make perfect sense to you as well. I promise.

Until that time, trust life. That is what your father in heaven invites you to do. Trust life, and love it. Live it fully, live it zestfully, live it happily.

Have fun.

Spread Joy.

Share love.

ARE THE PEOPLE/PSYCHICS/MEDIUMS THAT SAY THEY CAN TALK TO SPIRITS FOR REAL? WHY DON'T OUR DEPARTED LOVED ONES JUST CONTACT US DIRECTLY? *—Alex, 19*

They do, Alex. They do.

Now I don't want to get "strange" with you here, Alex, but let me use an example. Our friend Victoria, who asked the question above, *just received a communication from her father.*

Now she can believe that or not, as she wishes. It will not change the fact that her father *brought her here, to this book,* to tell her exactly what she needed to hear: that he is all right, that she will be all right, that everything is perfect just the way it worked out, and to be glad.

Do you think Victoria asked this question and came to this answer by accident?

Alex, there is no such thing as an accident.

OH, MAN.

Now to expand on my answer . . .

Loved ones who have "died" can be with you with the speed of your thought. In fact, they are. Instantly they come to you, with joy and great big smiles, showering you with their love. You can feel this, you can actually feel it, if you will let yourself, if you will open yourself to it.

But when you feel this energy of light and love, do not call it your imagination, nor label it wishful thinking. *It is the best kind of thinking you can do.*

269

Remember this always: *As you think, so will it be done unto you.*

If you think that your loved ones are with you—especially in times of need, when you could really use their advice—you will open yourself to the experience of the truth that they *are* there, and were, the moment you called them.

Yet if you think that they are not there, that you are "making it all up," then the truth that the essence of who they are is surrounding you will be lost to you; you will not be able to experience it.

BUT WHAT ABOUT MEDIUMS AND PSYCHICS? WOULDN'T IT BE EASIER TO USE THEM IF THEY ARE REALLY ABLE TO COMMUNICATE WITH SPIRITS?

All of you are able to communicate with spirits. That is what I have been telling you. You do not need a medium or a psychic to make it easy, and that does not mean that they cannot make it easy. It means you do not need them in order to do so.

But let's get clear here what we mean by "spirits." I am not talking about what are popularly referred to as "ghosts." When I use the word "spirit" I am referring to that part of a person that is also sometimes called the "soul."

THE "SPIRIT" IS THE SAME AS THE "SOUL"?

Yes. You have heard it said that you are a three-part being, made up of body, mind, and spirit. That third aspect of you is your soul. This is the essence of Who You Are. It is the most basic element of you. It is from spirit that everything emerges, and to spirit that everything returns.

All of you can get in touch with your own soul, and then, with the souls of others. It will be very difficult to do the second, however, unless you have done the first.

You will find it a challenge to contact or experience or become sensitive to the presence of another soul if you have not contacted, experienced, or become sensitive to the presence of your own.

WHY?

Because it is at the soul level that contact is made. The soul is the part of you that is connected to everything else. The body is the part of you that is separate.

The mind is the bridge between the two.

HOW CAN I USE MY MIND TO FIND MY SOUL?

Through the avenue of your thoughts. You must first believe that you *have* a soul. You must begin to see yourself as who and what you really are: a spirit, living with a body, and using a mind.

Remember this always: *Your body is not who you are. It is something you have. Your mind is not who you are, it is something you use. Your soul is the essence of who you are.*

Use your mind, but use it only briefly. Use your mind just long enough to tell yourself that you have a soul, that the search is worthwhile, that who you are is not your body or your mind. Then, get *out* of your mind. *Drop* your thoughts. *Clear your head* and move into your experience.

HOW DO I DO *THAT?*

There are many ways. Quiet contemplation and prayer are extremely effective, and that is why in monasteries and convents members of religious orders do both.

I THOUGHT PEOPLE IN MONASTERIES AND CONVENTS WERE TRYING TO GET IN TOUCH WITH GOD.

They are. When they get in touch with their own soul, God is who they DO get in touch with. And the reverse is also true.

SO I HAVE TO LIVE LIKE A MONK OR A NUN IN ORDER TO CONNECT WITH MY SOUL?

No. That is just one way. You can create moments of quiet contemplation or prayer in your own life if you wish. It might seem difficult at first if your life is very active, which is true for many young people, but with determination it can become enjoyable and easy.

I DON'T KNOW HOW TO TELL YOU THIS, BUT I AM NOT REALLY INTO PRAYER.

Prayer is simply having an earnest desire for something. Did you know that?

NO, I DIDN'T.

Well, then this should be good news. Every earnest hope or desire is a prayer. Maybe it is simply a desire to say thanks. Or a hope of things to come. But if you really wish to know God, and if you really wish to become aware of your own soul, that "wish," that feeling of inner desire, is all the "prayer" you need.

Now you can actually *say a prayer* if you choose to—that has often been helpful to many people—but it is not something that you *have to do*. It is simply a way of verbalizing in your mind what your heart already knows.

OKAY, I GET THAT. BUT I'M ALSO NOT INTO THIS "QUIET CONTEMPLATION" STUFF. I MEAN, I DON'T TAKE MANY LONG WALKS ALONE IN THE WOODS, YOU KNOW?

Do you ever lie around all by yourself and listen to music?

SURE! SO YOU'RE TELLING ME THAT LISTENING TO MY CDS IS "QUIET CONTEMPLATION"?

It can be. The word "quiet" when used in the phrase "quiet contemplation" doesn't necessarily have to mean "silent." It can mean that you *quiet the mind to everything else but the thing you are contemplating*.

What you focus on during moments of solitude can have a deep effect on you—especially if you focus on it over and over again. So be selective about what you focus on over and over again.

For instance, as you pick out the music you want to listen to, notice what it is inviting you to give your focus to. Watch the energies that it brings up. If the music has lyrics, read the words. See where the song is "taking" you. Is this where you want to "be"?

Don't make a judgment about it being "good" or "bad" (and don't let anybody else do so). Just ask yourself, is this the energy that I want to focus on?

If you focus on your soul—whether you use music or some other means—you'll find it. You'll discover it. Of course, you're not really "finding" or "discovering" anything, you're simply becoming aware of what has always been there.

CAN YOU TELL ME MORE ABOUT THE "OTHER MEANS"?

Sure.

Writing in your journal is a good way to focus on your soul; it's a good way to "discover" or "find" your real self, to get in touch with your real feelings, to clarify your real truth.

Another means of focusing on the soul is meditation.

I've mentioned this before, and we've talked about walking, or riding your bike, and other ways to remove your attention from the day-to-day activities and concerns of your life. This is a process of emptying your mind so that your spirit can fill in the space.

There are a lot of ways you can experience your soul. All you have to do is *get into the spirit of things*.

HEY, I LIKE THAT. THAT WAS A NEAT WAY OF PUT-TING IT.

Thanks.

BUT WE GOT OFF THE SUBJECT HERE. I WAS TALK-ING ABOUT PSYCHICS AND STUFF, AND HOW IT MIGHT BE EASIER FOR THEM THAN IT IS FOR US TO CONTACT SPIRITS. WHAT I WANT TO KNOW IS, ARE THEY FOR REAL?

Psychics and mediums are not unusual peo-ple who have unique abilities, but people just like you, whose abilities are in no way different from yours.

Indeed, this is how you can tell if a psychic is, as you put it, "for real." A true psychic will never try to convince you that they have abilities you do not have. Indeed, they will tell you that it is *your* ability to connect with the loved ones you hold dear that they are using when they do a "reading" for you.

Psychics simply act as amplifiers of the *"signal" that you are receiving.* They are being sensitive to *you,* not to some other energy or being. They have become, quite literally, the "loudspeaker" for the still small voice of wisdom and clarity and connectedness that lies within *you.*

You do not need a psychic or a medium to feel the presence and experience the love and receive the messages of loved ones who have died. It is also true that people who are sensitive to these energies can sometimes help you to feel them. That is why psychics are frequently called "sensitives."

You can sensitize yourself to these energies, and in this answer I've given you some hints on how.

WHEN IS IT MY TIME TO GO UP TO HEAVEN?
—*Chris, Miami, Florida*

You are in heaven right now, Chris. Heaven can be experienced wherever you are, and the sad thing is that everyone does not know this.

"Heaven on Earth" is experiencing all the wonders, all the joys, all the thrills, all the excitement, and all the happiness of life just as you're living it. You need nothing more than what I have given you to be in paradise. Your planet *is* a paradise, and all you have to do is open your eyes to see that.

Now if what you are asking me, Chris, is when you are going to die, I cannot tell you, because that is a decision that you are going to make.

When you see and experience that the conditions are perfect for it, that is when you will do it, and not a moment before, and not a moment after. And that will be your choice, not mine.

YOU KEEP SAYING THAT! BUT IT DOESN'T FEEL LIKE I'M GETTING TO CHOOSE ANYTHING! IT SEEMS LIKE LIFE IS "HAPPENING" TO ME!

Change your mind about that! You are co-creating what is happening, along with everyone else around you. That is what I have been telling you here.

You can change what you are experiencing by changing what you are thinking. Then change what you are saying. Then change what you are doing.

This is the three-part Process of Creation. It is the most powerful tool you will ever be given.

OKAY, I GET IT. I REALLY DO GET IT. BUT YOU'RE NOT ANSWERING THE MOST IMPORTANT QUESTION I HAVE ABOUT DEATH. *WHY DO WE EVEN HAVE TO DIE? WHY CAN'T WE LIVE FOREVER?*

You can and do live forever! You never do die. That is what I am telling you here. You live on, merely changing form.

OKAY, OKAY, BUT YOU KNOW WHAT I MEAN. WHY DO WE HAVE TO LEAVE THE BODY THAT WE ARE WITH RIGHT NOW?

I never said you had to do that. The human race has chosen to do that, by the way people have treated their bodies, and their environment, and by the way they have lived their lives.

You can stay with your body a lot longer than you might ever have thought possible. You can

279

do this by taking—individually, and as a society—some of the suggestions I have given you already.

Yet, I invite you not to consider your departure from the body—what you call "death"—a fearful or unwelcome experience. It does not have to be either.

DEATH IS NOT FEARFUL OR UNWELCOME?

Not unless you choose for it to be. As with the rest of your life, everything depends upon your point of view. Your perspective shapes your experience.

If you are afraid of "what will happen to you" after your death, you will be afraid of death. If you think that death is the end of life, you will be afraid of its arrival.

If, on the other hand, you are clear about what will happen to you after your death, you will be at peace about it. There may be a trace of sadness, but there can also be a balancing excitement—like going on to college, or changing jobs, or moving to a new city.

YOU'RE COMPARING DEATH TO GOING TO COLLEGE, CHANGING JOBS, OR MOVING TO A NEW CITY?

Well, I was just using a simile—a comparison, so that you could understand the feeling—but, come to think of it, it's very much like those things.

And when you know that death is not the end of life, but that life goes on forever, you no longer find this experience of transition unwelcome.

BUT WHERE I WILL BE GOING, HEAVEN OR HELL?

Yes, that is the question that worries so many. So let us take the worry out of it once and for all.

You will be coming home, to me.

As we have discussed before here, there is no such place as hell.

BUT YOU SAID EARLIER THAT THERE IS AN *EXPERIENCE* OF HELL, WHICH YOU SAID WAS THE EXPERIENCE OF SEPARATION FROM GOD.

Yes. That's good. You are really following the conversation here. So now let me explain what happens to you at the moment of your death.

ALL RIGHT! NOW WE'RE GETTING TO IT!

What you experience is whatever you wish or choose or expect to experience. As in physical life, your spiritual life will be created by you—by your own thoughts, ideas, and beliefs.

SO IF I THINK I AM GOING TO HELL, I *WILL* GO TO HELL!

You could create a hellish experience, that is true, but you've done that on Earth as well and survived it. So, too, could it be in what you call the Afterlife. And the moment you decide that you no longer choose your hell-like experience, you can stop it. Then you will know that you are truly in heaven, where you may experience anything you wish with the speed of your thought.

 WHAT DOES HEAVEN LOOK LIKE?
                        —Anne, 15, Indianapolis, Indiana

Whatever you choose for it to look like.

 WHEN WILL I GET TO SEE YOU IN HEAVEN?
                        —Roberto, 14

Whenever you wish.

HOW IS HEAVEN? DO WE MEET THE ONES WE LOST WHEN WE PASS AWAY?

—Fernando, 16

At the moment of your death you will be surrounded by your loved ones gone before, who will lovingly and joyfully guide you. You will experience them being there if you wish.

WHAT DOES THAT MEAN?

It means that you will experience your loved ones all around you if you choose to, and if you do not expect to and do not think that you will, you will not experience them there. They will be there, but you will not experience them there. They will be loving you and guiding you all the same, and when you choose to, you will experience them there.

It is the same way during your life on Earth. Your departed loved ones surround you with the speed of your thought. If you are open to the experience, you will know they are there.

It is the same way, by the way, with God. Both in this life, and even forever more.

18

Other Mysteries

Now here are a few questions that did not seem to fit into any one category. I wanted to include them in the book because—well, first of all, because you asked them, and secondly, because I thought they were interesting and deserved an individual response. Yet, since these are not all about a particular subject, the topics hop all over the place. Have fun with this, and enjoy the various questions and responses.

TO ME, LIFE IS POINTLESS. I MEAN, IT IS COMPLETELY POINTLESS. ANY COMMENT?

—Nick, 18

Yes. You're right. Life IS pointless. That's the point of it.

OKAY, YOU'VE GOT MY INTEREST. . . .

There is no point to life except the point you give it. If life had some point to it, who would be the one to have said what that point is? And if you say, "God," why would I do that and then keep everything secret?

Do you really think that there is some point to life that I have assigned it, and that I then make you hunt around for it for the rest of your life? Is that your imagining?

YOU HAVEN'T MADE US HUNT AROUND FOR IT. YOU'VE SPELLED IT OUT FOR US.

Where?

IN THE HOLY SCRIPTURE.

Which Holy Scripture?

285

YOU KNOW PERFECTLY WELL WHICH HOLY SCRIPTURE.

No, I don't. I don't know which one you are referring to. Is it the Bible? Is it the Koran? Is it the Talmud? Is it the Upanishads, or the Book of Mormon? Is it the Pali Canon, or the Bhagavad Gita, or the Tao-te Ching? Could it be the Rig Veda, or the Brahmanas, or the Buddha-Dharma?

OKAY, OKAY, I GET THE POINT.

Do you? I mean, do you, really? Because, you know, there are hundreds of known religions on the planet, and each has its teachings and its scriptures. Which one should we choose to be the one and only Word of God?

THE ONE I CHOOSE!

Yes, of course. And what is the point of life, according to the scripture that you choose?

WELL, LIKE I SAID, TO ME LIFE HAS NO POINT, SO I GUESS MAYBE YOU DIDN'T TELL US AFTER ALL. WHY NOT TELL US RIGHT HERE AND SAVE US ALL THE FRUSTRATION?

I am telling you right here! I am telling you that you are right. Life is pointless. If it had some point to it, given by me, you would have no choice but to use your life to make that point. Yet I created you to create, not to obey. God obeys no one, and I made you in the image and likeness of me.

So, life was made pointless *on purpose*, in order for you to be free to give it whatever point you choose to give it. You do this, as an individual and as a society, every day.

WE DO? WE ARE DOING THIS EVERY DAY?

Yes. You are declaring what the point of life is by your behavior. Your behavior is something that *you can control,* and the behavior of other humans is something that *you can influence.*

 IS THERE A CURE FOR CANCER?   *—Barbi*

Yes, Barbi. And for AIDS. And for multiple sclerosis, muscular dystrophy, Alzheimer's disease, and every other illness you can mention.

You can heal yourself of these things in three ways.

First, by preventing them from occurring. (This can be done in any number of ways, from changing your life habits to changing your genetic coding at birth.)

Second, by repairing any organs and tissues damaged by diseases that were not prevented. (This can be done by using the human body's own cells to regenerate and actually "rebuild" damaged body parts.)

Third, by the simple power of faith. That is, by asking for a healing and "knowing of a certainty" that you are going to get it.

In the years ahead, your species will come to understand all of this. In fact, one day it will all seem very simple.

IF THERE IS A CURE FOR THESE THINGS, OR A WAY TO HEAL THEM, WHY NOT TELL US ABOUT IT RIGHT NOW? WHY MAKE US WAIT FOR YEARS AND YEARS? WHAT KIND OF A GOD WOULD DO THAT?

Not me, for sure. And I am not doing that. Everything you need to know to cure disease and heal the body is encoded in the body itself.

I have given you the textbook. You are the textbook. Study how the body works, look closely at its mechanisms. Examine the miracle cells that can turn themselves into any part of the body, from bones to heart muscle to brain tissue. Look closely, as you are now doing, at the genetic code of humans, and at all of life. You are even now unlocking life's secrets.

BUT WHY HAVE WE HAD TO WAIT SO LONG? WHY DIDN'T YOU SHOW US THESE THINGS SOONER?

Life reveals itself to life completely, in every moment. It is not a matter of how much is revealed, but how much is believed.

For example, it was observable from the beginning that the Earth revolved around the sun. Your species simply did not want to believe it.

Some people actually *did* observe that the Earth revolves around the sun, but when they said so in public, it created a huge theological debate, mainly because it violated spiritual teaching at the time, which insisted that human beings were God's highest creatures, and that, therefore, the sun must revolve around the Earth!

Many other scientific and medical discoveries have likewise been dismissed, if not condemned, on your planet because they violated what humans imagined that they already knew on the subject, or because it shook the foundation of their already-in-place religious beliefs.

They would rather have held onto their beliefs—even if mistaken—than adopt a new point of view on things that challenged those beliefs.

LIKE YOU SAID EARLIER, SOME PEOPLE WILL GIVE UP EVERYTHING TO BE "RIGHT." EVEN PROGRESS.

Exactly. And the human race is in much the same position today. For that reason this very book will be put down by some. The idea that God would communicate directly with you—to say nothing of *what* is being communicated here—violates nearly every religious belief that most of your societies hold.

Yet I will tell you something. Everything that has been written here will one day become commonly accepted.

Unless it's not.

You are creating your reality, and you will decide how you choose your world to be.

Do you choose a world in which God talks to you plainly and simply, answering your questions directly, and giving you tools with which to change your life?

Do you choose a world in which disease can be eradicated forever, and illness can be a thing of the past?

Do you choose a planet that is environmentally safe, with resources that have not been depleted?

Do you imagine that these ideas can be your reality? If you do, they can. If you do not, they cannot.

It is as simple as that.

? **HOW CAN I USE MY HURTS AND DISAP-POINTMENTS TO MAKE ME THE BEST I CAN POSSIBLY BE? CAN I USE THEM AS STEPPING-STONES TO A BETTER PLACE, RATHER THAN AS OBSTACLES THAT HOLD ME BACK OR RESTRICT ME FROM BEING THE PERSON I CAN BE AND DOING THE THINGS I WANT TO ACCOMPLISH?** *—Iana, 16*

You can, indeed—and what a wonderful question to ask!

First, you must change the way you look at things. You must understand that I have sent you nothing but angels, and that I have brought you nothing but miracles.

Then you must remember that "failure" is an illusion. In truth, it is not possible to fail at anything.

Remember this always: *you cannot fail*.

When you feel hurt, or experience disappointment, allow yourself to see this as a gift, and open it up to find the treasure within.

Let nothing become an obstacle. *Nothing*. Know that you may have or experience anything that you wish, if you but believe.

Know most of all that all things are happening for your highest good, always. Even when it "looks like" you are not receiving what you choose, you are.

Remember that, at some level of consciousness, you have brought every encounter and experience to you, for reasons that are perfectly in alignment with the agenda of your soul.

In this sense, everything is something you have "wished for," and you are always getting what you want. When you know and understand this, you have reached mastery in living.

Call each moment a blessing—even moments of hurt and disappointment—and, using this power to see things the way you *choose* to see things, rob those moments of any suffering. They may be painful, but they do not have to involve any suffering.

Learn to *welcome* defeat as merely a rung on the ladder of success. Indeed, do not see it as "defeat" at all, but as *victory of another sort*.

When you see the gift that life has given you in the grandest sorrows and in the deepest tragedies, then you are Christed; you become as The Buddha. There is an implacability, which cannot be disrupted. There is a peacefulness, which it is impossible to destroy. There is *a joy endless*.

 IS IT UNGODLY TO WANT REVENGE ON SOME-ONE?
—Larysa, 19, Mississauga, Ontario, Canada

The human race has long believed in a vengeful God and by this means justified its own vengeful spirit. Far from seeing themselves as made in the image and likeness of God, humans think that God is made in the image and likeness of humans.

I do not need revenge, nor do I seek it. As I explained earlier, this is because I cannot be hurt or damaged in any way.

If you believe that you can be hurt or damaged in any way, you are already acting "ungodly," whether you seek revenge or not. The very act of thinking that you *need* revenge is an identification of yourself as something less than God—and hence, "ungodly."

The answer to your question is, therefore, yes.

Do not, however, "beat yourself up" for having these feelings—nor for anything that you have ever felt or done. You have simply forgotten Who You Really Are.

As you remember your true identity you will see that it is not necessary to feel guilty or "make yourself wrong" for whatever "ungodly" things you may have thought, said, or done.

You will understand that it is all part of the process of evolution—of your own growth, of the evolution of your species, and of your own soul.

You will see, therefore, that you have never "failed," but only taken steps toward your own success.

 WHY ARE THERE BOTH WHITE AND BLACK PEOPLE?   *—Anonymous*

The technical reasons are not important. These simply have to do with the pigmentation or color of the skin that was developed and required by the process of human evolution as it took place in various locations on the Earth.

These are not the real reasons at all, but merely describe the *process* by which the real reasons are made manifest in your reality.

For example, driving your car may be the technical reason you are able to get to the grocery store. The real reason you are *going*, however, is to get bread, butter, eggs, and milk. You've created the car (and many other inventions) as a device or a tool with which you may carry out your intentions—which are your real reasons for using these tools.

Life in the physical body, and the *evolution of that life*, is the device that souls have used to carry out their intentions.

People are black and white (and other shades as well) for the same reason they are male and female, short and tall, gay and straight, left-handed and right-handed. You have used the tool of genetics to create *differences* between you, because in the absence of that which you are not, that which you are is not.

HELP ME TO UNDERSTAND THAT AGAIN. I DON'T THINK I UNDERSTAND THAT.

In order to experience yourself in a certain way, you need to create another way to be experienced. Then and only then can you know

295

yourself as a particular individualization of The Whole—a singular and specific presentation of All That Is.

Without cold there cannot be warm, without up there cannot be down . . .

OH, YEAH. I REMEMBER THAT NOW.

You are a human snowflake.

You fall from God's heaven as an awesomely individual, no-two-alike expression of the Wonder of Life.

When you arrive on Earth you merge with others who, like you, are each breathtakingly unique, yet who together form a beautiful picture of a larger kind.

Eventually you change form, melting into one body, flowing easily and effortlessly in a stream of oneness.

Finally you seem to disappear (although you are there, you simply cannot be seen) as you rise back to the heavens whence you came, to begin the cycle all over again.

The Journey of the Snowflake is a perfect metaphor for the journey of the soul.

WHAT IF "MATING FOR LIFE" IS NOT THE WAY THINGS ARE SUPPOSED TO BE, BUT JUST THE WAY WE HAVE *DECIDED* THEY ARE SUPPOSED TO BE? IS IT OKAY TO LIVE WITH SOMEBODY WITHOUT HAVING TO MAKE A LIFELONG COMMITMENT TO HIM?

—Susan, 19, St. Louis, Missouri

There is no rule in the heavens that says you must remain with a person for the rest of your life in order to be with them now.

BUT . . . WHAT IF I WANT TO LIVE WITH HIM AS . . . YOU KNOW . . . AS MAN AND WIFE?

You mean you want to have sex with him. You want to sleep with him.

NOT *JUST* THAT, BUT YES, THAT. I LOVE HIM AND I WANT TO DO EVERYTHING WITH HIM; LIVE WITH HIM, EAT WITH HIM, SLEEP WITH HIM, SHARE DAY-TO-DAY LIFE WITH HIM. I'M JUST NOT SURE I'M READY TO GET MARRIED. BUT MY PARENTS THINK I SHOULD. THEY DO MORE THAN *THINK* I SHOULD,

THEY *SAY* I SHOULD, POINT-BLANK. IN FACT, THEY SAY THAT IF I DON'T, I'LL BE LIVING IN SIN.

And just who will you be sinning against?

YOU, I GUESS. IT'S A SIN AGAINST GOD.

Really? You think that I will be offended if you are loving someone?

WELL, NOT JUST LOVING THEM, *LIVING WITH THEM*.

Yes, I understand.

I MEAN, MOVING IN WITH HIM RAISES THE LEVEL OF INTIMACY, DON'T YOU THINK?

You have not been intimate with this person?

WELL, YES, IT'S HAPPENED A FEW TIMES, BUT THAT'S NOT THE SAME AS ACTUALLY LIVING WITH HIM.

Are you saying that it is okay to share an intimate relationship so long as you each have your own place, but that if you share the same place, then it is not okay?

NO, BUT . . . IT JUST MAKES IT MORE OBVIOUS, I GUESS. EVERYTHING BECOMES SO . . . OPEN . . . AND UNDENIABLE.

It sounds to me as though it may be *appearances* that you are worried about, not sin. Most people do what they really want to do, and when they think that others might object, they simply do it in secret.

Perhaps you are more worried about offending humans than about offending God.

WELL, THERE'S SUCH A THING AS A SMALL SIN . . . A LITTLE SLIPUP, A MOMENT OF GIVING IN TO PASSION . . . AND THEN THERE'S THE BIGGER SIN OF DOING SOMETHING OVER AND OVER AGAIN, KNOWING THAT IT'S WRONG AND JUST, WELL, *DEFYING GOD.*

I see. So a sin committed one or two times—or in your case, fifteen or twenty—is forgivable, but a sin committed every day of the month, all year long, is not.

I'M SUDDENLY SOUNDING SILLY HERE.

No, Susan, I'm the one who's sounding silly. Some human beings make it sound as if God will look the other way as long as they are doing what they are doing discreetly, in hiding, but that if they do the same thing openly, with everyone clear about what is happening, then God will be offended and have to punish them.

They make me sound like the I.R.S.

Now here is the good news, Susan. I am not offended and I am not going to punish you if you love someone, whether it is in your home, in their home, or in a home you create together, however spontaneously or impermanently.

It is not my place to judge and to punish you, Susan, and I will never do that. It is not my place to "make you wrong," and then to "make you pay." Everyone wants to assign me that task, but I am not accepting it.

It is my job to love you, Susan. Plainly and simply, to love you. To love you now, and forevermore. To love you no matter what.

I understand how you could want to live with this man. I understand how you could love him. And I understand how you could nevertheless be unsure about whether you want to spend the rest of your life with him. I understand every feeling you have about that. And when understanding comes, condemnation goes.

Remember that always: *When understanding comes, condemnation goes.*

Understanding and condemnation are mutually exclusive.

I NEVER HEARD ANYONE SAY THAT BEFORE.

Well, you're hearing it now, and it's true.

BUT WHAT *ABOUT* MARRIAGE? WHAT IS THE PLACE OF MARRIAGE IN OUR SOCIETY TODAY?

Marriage is an institution that humans created and a state into which they enter, in order, they say, to sanctify their love. Does this mean that love expressed outside of marriage is not sanctified? That is something only you can decide.

You are in the process of defining yourself, as a person and as a society. You do so with every decision that you make.

So, think about what your mother says, think about what your heart says, think about what your soul says to you about love. But of this one thing be sure: do not make your decision— about this or any other thing—based on fear.

And know that the thing to be least afraid of is me.

Strive to have a Friendship with God, not a Fearship with God. Think of me as your best friend. Come to me always, as you have here, with your questions, with your concerns, with your hopes and dreams, and know that I will be with you always. Not to judge you or condemn you, but to help you experience the grandest version of the greatest vision you ever held about Who You Are!

? **I WEAR A CRUCIFIX AROUND MY NECK AS A GOOD LUCK CHARM. SO FAR, IT HASN'T BROUGHT ME MUCH LUCK. LOTS OF MY FRIENDS WEAR THEM, TOO. IT'S A SIGN OF MY FAITH. WHY ISN'T IT WORKING?**

—Manuel, 14, Manila, Philippines

Good luck charms do not bring good luck. Intention and pure knowing is what produces positive outcomes in life.

You do not demonstrate your faith by wearing a crucifix, any more than you do so by going to church or to synagogue or to temple every day or every week. You demonstrate your faith by every word that you utter. By every thought that you hold. By everything that you do.

It is your thoughts, words, and actions that create your reality, not something that you wear or carry with you.

I invite you to look to see if it has worked to put faith in things. Then I invite you to put faith in yourself. Put faith in the process of *life*. And put faith in God.

You and life and God are not at odds with each other. You are all on the same side, all on one team.

It goes further than that. You and life and God are all *the same thing*. You are what life is, life is what God is, God is what you are. The circle is complete.

So, have faith in all of that! Don't worry about "good luck charms." *Life* is your good luck charm. To make it work, *know* that it will work, *say* that it will work, *act as if* it will work. And do you know what? *It will work.*

Life will work out in the process of life itself. Remember that always: *Life works out in the process of life itself.*

WILL I EVER BE ABLE TO SEE ANGELS?

—Avra

Absolutely, Avra. You can see them right now! Just open your eyes and look around. Everyone in your life is an angel. *I have sent you nothing but angels.*

They have come into your life to play their right and perfect parts. Some of them "show up" in one way, some in another, but all are there for your soul's purpose.

Yet you do not even have to leave your house to see an angel. You can see an angel by looking in the mirror. Yes, you are an angel. Are you able to accept that?

I invite you to seriously consider this: What would it be like if you thought that you were *the angel someone else is waiting for today?*

I can tell you what it would be like.

You would change everyone whose life you touch.

They would truly have been . . . "touched by an angel."

HOW CAN I DO THIS? WHAT WOULD I HAVE TO DO?

It is not about doing anything in particular. It is about being. When you move into your Angel Self you are "being," not "doing."

WHAT AM I BEING?

You are being whatever you imagine an angel to be. Perhaps you are being loving. Perhaps you are being compassionate, and patient, and kind. Perhaps you are being generous, and helpful, and caring, and sensitive, and understanding, and forgiving, and protecting, and encouraging, and guiding. And perhaps you are being willing.

WILLING?

Yes, willing.

WILLING FOR WHAT? WILLING TO DO WHAT?

Willing to do whatever those states of being bring up for you to do.

Willing to allow whatever you are doing to bubble up, to spring forth, from those ways of being.

Willing not to think about it, not to consider the "pros and cons," not to worry about the balance sheet, not to weigh what you're going to get out of it.

Willing to just do what will come naturally to do when you are being those things, moment to moment.

The present moment will tell you what to do when you are a human *being*. You won't have to think about it.

Remember this about the present moment. It is, in fact, just that—the *pre-sent moment*. It was *sent to you in advance* by your soul, to allow you to express and experience who you really are, and who you now choose to be.

The present moment is also the "present" moment. It is the moment when a "present" is given and received. What gift will you give to another, and to yourself, in this "present" moment?

That is the only question to ask today.

Yet do not think about the answer. BE the answer.

Remember this always: *Angels never think.*

WILL I EVER BE ABLE TO SEE "ANGELIC" ANGELS, AND NOT JUST "EARTH ANGELS"? I MEAN, LIKE THE ANGELS IN HEAVEN?

You have no doubt seen many of them already.

I HAVE?

Yes. They would have appeared to you as ordinary human beings. They've moved in and out of your life, bringing you just what you needed, just when you've needed it.

You have also no doubt encountered them in your dreams, which is where your soul goes to rest between days of carrying around the body.

They have appeared to you in many forms while you are in this state.

WILL I SEE THEM WHEN I GO TO HEAVEN?

At the moment that you leave your body, they will be all around you, showering you with love. It is their energy that will be the first energy that you feel as you move through your transition.

WHAT WILL THAT FEEL LIKE?

It will feel warm, soft, welcoming, and safe. Safety will be the main feeling. Total safety and absolute love.

WOW, I CAN'T WAIT.

You don't have to wait! The good news is that you never have to wait, not for the love of angels, and not for the love and presence of God.

You can feel this anytime that you wish.

WHY IS IT THAT I CAN DIE FOR MY COUNTRY AT 18, BUT I CAN'T ENJOY A COLD BEER ON A HOT DAY?

Older adults often feel that their offspring "belong" to them, and are to do as they say. Society in general reflects this "we own your body" point of view. Therefore, society believes it has a right to tell its offspring what to do.

Your society feels it has a perfect right to send you into a war that you may not even agree with, but to keep you out of a bar with which you do.

Your society has even passed laws *forcing* you to do one, while prohibiting you from doing the other, or face penalties and possible imprisonment.

This is a reflection of the primitiveness of your society. No enlightened society would presume, under color of law, to have the right to order your body around in such a manner, regardless of the will of your own person.

Not too long ago, societies felt they had the

same right regarding females. In some countries they still do.

Societies in these countries dictate what women can and cannot do, where they can and cannot work, who they can and cannot marry, what they can and cannot wear (right down to the color of the cloth), where they can and cannot go, and at what hours of the day or night they may or may not venture there.

Some of these repressive societies even deform the bodies of females, forcing them to have portions of their genitalia removed (the portions that bring females pleasure during intercourse), because for a female to experience pleasure during intercourse is considered inappropriate.

Yes, your human societies have created laws that are not only unfair, but cross the borders of sanity.

WHY? WHY DO WE PASS SUCH LAWS?

This question was asked earlier, and I did not answer it head on. It is because humans live in fear and guilt. Fear and guilt are the only enemies of man.

When you live in fear and guilt, you are

forced to seek total control of your environment, and of everyone in it. Power and control are what become important.

Other people expressing their free will are seen, to varying degrees in varying countries, as threats to the common good. The "common good" is, of course, defined by those in power.

WHAT COULD PEOPLE IN THOSE COUNTRIES YOU TALKED ABOUT POSSIBLY FEAR FROM WOMEN THAT WOULD MAKE THEM PASS SUCH CRUEL LAWS?

Self-discovery. Self-realization. Self-awareness.

If women are allowed to experience Who They Really Are, the men in those countries will no longer be able to control them.

Why do you think it took so long, even in your so-called "advanced and enlightened" countries, to grant women the simple right to vote?

It is about control. Always it is about control. And always, this control masquerades as something that is needed, something that is "for the good of the people." Yet *freedom* is the only thing that is desired by the human soul, for that is what the human soul IS, and what it always seeks to express. Anything less than the granting of total freedom is not for the "good of the people," but for the good of those in power.

YOU'RE RIGHT! I FEEL THAT ADULTS ARE ALWAYS TRYING TO CONTROL *US*. WHAT'S ALL THIS ABOUT? WHY ALL THESE POWER TRIPS?

Most of the human race has not yet learned how to use power. Most of the people do not understand the concept of power WITH, but only of power OVER.

Remember this always: *The purpose of power is not to control, but to create.*

When power is used to control, it creates nothing. That is why individuals who are "control freaks" have a very hard time making things happen, and governments that control accomplish even less.

Control is the enemy of creation.

"Controlled creation" is an oxymoron.

The totally creative person is often said to be "totally out of control." It is true! That person is! And that person *couldn't create anything if he or she were not*.

True freedom is true power. That is the state of being in which God resides. It is the state of being in which humans reside as well, but they do not know it.

We have now come full circle in this book. With these last two questions we have explored what we discussed at the beginning of this conversation.

You are all born with Original Power.

This is simply another term for God.

When you reclaim Original Power, you reclaim God. You reclaim your divinity. Divinity exercises power *with*, not *over*, the universe.

That last sentence, that one single sentence, clears up the most basic misunderstanding humans have about God.

Original Power is what IS. This power forms and supports every law of the universe, including the law of creation. It is the law of life, and the law of God.

All of the prophets have told you this. Today's modern-day prophets say it in their own way, yet the new way they say it does not change the law, but simply clarifies it.

Here is the law: Ultimate power is ultimate freedom, and ultimate freedom is ultimate power.

Sharing power does not diminish power, it increases it.

Do not think I have come to abolish the law and prophets. I have not come to abolish them, but to fulfill them.

Now you know.

I have not come here to exercise power *over* you, but to exercise power *with* you.

There is a world of difference, and you will live in a different world when you understand this.

 ONE LAST QUESTION ABOUT GOD. IF YOU MADE US, THEN WHO MADE YOU?

—Luciano, 14, Rome, Italy

That is a wonderful question, Luciano, because it focuses on one of the great mysteries of the universe.

Nobody "made" me, Luciano. I am life itself. I am that which is, that which was, and that which always will be. There was never a time that I was not.

313

You, Luciano, are the same thing. You always were, are now, and always will be. That is because you and I are one. What I am, you are. What you are, I am. We are the same thing. We are life, expressing. We are That Which Is, being.

I am the sum total of all of It, and you are the part of It now expressing itself as Luciano. Yet we are not separate from each other in any way.

When you stop expressing yourself as Luciano (that is, when you do the thing that you call "die"), you will continue to live and express yourself as a part of me. You cannot not do this, for you are a part of who I am, and there is no part of me that can ever end.

And so your life will go on, Luciano, forever. You may keep the identity of "Luciano" after you leave your present body for as long as you wish, and you will do so for as long as it serves you.

When it no longer serves you to know yourself as Luciano, you will meld into The Oneness and be the part of me that has no individual identity. This melding into The Oneness is what some humans have termed Nirvana. It is the extinction of desire and individual consciousness.

THAT DOES NOT SOUND GOOD TO ME. WON'T I ALWAYS WANT TO HAVE DESIRES AND INDIVIDUAL CONSCIOUSNESS?

When you are One with Everything you will have no desires because *you are that from which all desires spring*. In a sense, desire is not desirable, nor even possible, for you already are that which you would desire.

Thus, desire as a "yearning" is eliminated from your experience. So is want, and need. You've become both the "wanter" and the "wanted," the "needer" and the "needed." In this state of total unity you want and need nothing.

This is pure bliss. It is the highest heaven.

There, you are in harmony with, *and become part of*, the Primal Vibration, the sound of Aum, the call of life.

Stimulated by this vibration, you will begin to differentiate once again. You will begin to separate from The All, becoming a specific and individual part of The Whole.

WHY? WHY CAN'T I STAY WITH THE ALL? WHY CAN'T I REMAIN IN THE BLISS?

The ongoing process of unification and differentiation is the Basic Process of Life Itself. It is occurring everywhere in the universe, at multiple levels and dimensions.

The Basic Process does not require you to abandon bliss. Indeed, it is bliss Itself. You may

315

experience this bliss at any point or time in the process, simply by remembering Who You Are, and what is going on.

HOW CAN I DO THAT?

In many ways. Meditation. Prayer. Making love. Smelling a flower. Creating music. Kissing a baby. Drawing a picture. Baking a pie. Fixing the plumbing. Doing anything, *anything*, with joy. Living your life to the fullest. Walking the Three-Way Path. Have fun. Spread joy. Share love.

I GOT IT! THANKS! CAN YOU HELP ME UNDER-STAND THIS PROCESS A LITTLE MORE? I DON'T UNDERSTAND COMPLETELY THIS ONENESS THING, AND THEN . . . WHAT DID YOU CALL IT? "DIFFEREN-TIATION"?

Yes. That's when a part of something be-comes different, and no longer looks like the rest of what it is a part of. It's like when you get out of your band uniform. You're still a member of the band, but now you look differ-ent, you look more like the "individual you" than the "collective you" that you called "the band."

Think of this nondifferentiated part of life as the largest part of All That Is. Think of it as the nonindividualized pool of energy from which everything that is individual emerges.

This "pool" is what many humans call God. It is that from which everything flows. It is that from which everything is created in its differentiated form.

It is the stem cell of the universe.

WHAT'S A STEM CELL?

Listen to me. *Your own body contains the blueprint of the universe.* Your body chemistry holds the secret to the mechanisms of all of life. You've been carrying around the greatest secret of life in your own body, and looking for it everywhere else.

At the basis of everything in your body is what your medical biologists call "stem cells." These cells have two "God-like" qualities. First, *they are immortal.* Second, *they are "shape-shifters."*

WHAT?

It's true.

Most living cells divide a finite number of

times and then perish. Stem cells, on the other hand, can be cultured to divide indefinitely.

In other words, under the right conditions, *they can replicate themselves forever.*

They can also turn into any other cell type there is.

In other words, under the right conditions, *they can turn themselves into anything.*

ARE YOU KIDDING ME?

No. Humans have known about stem cells since the late 1800s. They knew then that these cells were, as your dictionaries put it, "unspecialized cells that give rise to differentiated cells."

Still, it took your species more than a hundred years to discover how to isolate these cells and stimulate them to take the specific form needed to produce specific parts of your body.

It is now possible for your medical science to produce, from pure stem cells, everything from bones to heart muscle to brain tissue.

And you are learning about other mysteries as well. You are learning about cloning, and genetic engineering, and you are decoding the genome, analyzing the DNA of human beings and other organisms.

Soon you will be able to identify the chromosomal location of every human gene and to determine each gene's precise chemical structure in order to understand its function in health and disease.

You are about to unlock the secret of eternal life.

WHOA . . .

Yes. Once again . . . *whoa*.

This conversation has included a lot of "whoas," and this is the biggest one.

We are talking here about the Basic Process of life itself. What you call "God" is the undifferentiated Pure Cell of all of Life. It is to the universe what the stem cell is to your body.

The secret of God is the mechanism inside your own body. It is the mechanism of all of life. From the beginning of time, mystics have said that when you understand yourself you will understand God. *This was meant physically as well as spiritually.*

You are about to discover this.

OH, MY GOD.

Exactly. That is exactly right. I could not have put it into better words myself. "Oh, my God" is exactly right.

Science and spirituality are coming together now, joining paths, as inevitably they must. This is a time of excitement the likes of which your parents, and your parents' parents, never dreamed.

Now you understand more than ever why you came to this book. And not only why you came to this book, but why you came to your body, on this planet, at this particular moment.

Never before in the long life of the human species—*never*—has any moment been so ripe with possibilities, so filled with challenges, so ready for clear and exciting vision.

You, and the other young people all around you, will be living the largest part of your lives in this cosmic moment. The older people among you are approaching it, but you *will be moving through it*.

You will be facing the moral and spiritual implications of all that I have just revealed. You will be deciding what all of this means.

Do you think that you came to this time and place by accident?

I tell you, you did not.

This is the most extraordinary time in human history, and you came here to share the excitement. *And to create it*.

19

A Final Question

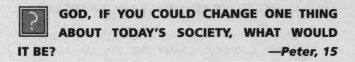

GOD, IF YOU COULD CHANGE ONE THING ABOUT TODAY'S SOCIETY, WHAT WOULD IT BE? —*Peter, 15*

I would change your beliefs about who you are, and who I am, and how life is.

I would cause you to notice that you and I are One, that you are likewise one with everything and everyone else, and that life is eternal, with no beginning and no end.

These simple ideas would alter the course of your experience forever, and change your whole world.

WHY DON'T YOU DO THAT, THEN? WHY DON'T YOU CAUSE US TO NOTICE THIS? WHY DON'T YOU CHANGE THIS ONE THING ABOUT OUR SOCIETY?

I do not do anything, Peter, on my own. If I did, I would be breaking the law of free will. I would be directly interfering in your life.

YOU WOULD BE VIOLATING THE "PRIME DIRECTIVE"!

Precisely.

SO THIS ONE THING WILL NEVER BE CHANGED?

There is only one way that this can occur, and that is through you. I cannot do it TO you, I can only do it THROUGH you. This is because Who You Are is me—God—expressed as life, in, as, and through YOU.

That is what I have come here to tell you.

That is what you have brought yourself here to be told. You, and everyone else who is holding this book in their hands.

HOW, THEN, CAN I CHANGE THE WORLD?

So far all the best efforts of your governments and your social systems and even your religions have not been able to change the most basic human behaviors. And so, after all this time, things are still pretty much the way they always have been among human beings—squabbling, fighting, killing, and inability to openly share or openly love.

WHY?

Because all humans do is keep trying to change the *conditions* of life on your planet, rather than the *beliefs that have created those conditions*.

Humans keep trying to eliminate the condition of poverty, the condition of hunger, the condition of misery, the condition of oppression, the condition of prejudice and lack of equal opportunity, the condition of violence, the condition of war . . . they keep trying to *make these conditions go away*.

323

They try religious persuasion; they try legislative mandate; they try royal decree; they try benevolent dictatorship; they try totalitarian government; they try popular uprising; they try everything they can think of, and still they cannot make these conditions go away.

With all humanity's supposed advancement, with all its fancy technology, with all of its newly created abundance and wealth, and with all its increased awareness, humans have not been able to eliminate the most basic problems of poverty, hunger, misery, oppression, prejudice and lack of equal opportunity, violence, and war.

And they *cannot*, because these conditions are *reflections of beliefs* that have not changed. If you want your world to change you have to work to change the world's beliefs.

Behaviors and conditions can only be changed temporarily. You may work on that now if you wish to provide temporary relief, but if you want long-term relief you must work on helping people change their beliefs.

Remember this always: *Beliefs create behaviors and behaviors create conditions*.

This is true in your individual life as well as in the collective reality that you are creating planetwide.

HOW CAN WE CHANGE BELIEFS? HOW CAN WE DO THAT?

First you have to be aware of what beliefs you are trying to change. Most people do not know what it is that they do believe. They have not thought about it deeply. They are too busy living. They are too busy trying to solve the problems *created* by their beliefs to look into the matter of what beliefs are creating them.

WHAT ARE THE BELIEFS WE NEED TO CHANGE?

The human race believes in neediness. It believes not only that there are things that it needs, it believes that it has insufficient means to meet those needs. It believes in disunity. It believes in failure. It believes in superiority.

It believes, most of all, in the conditionality of love. It believes that love is conditional. That my love is conditional, and that all love is conditional, and that, therefore, there are requirements that must be met in order to receive the benefits of love, and judgments that must be made about who has and who has not met those requirements, and condemnations that must be meted out to those who have failed.

Because it deeply believes in such a system of separateness, scarcity, failure, judgment, condemnation, and superiority, it allows itself to *behave in accordance with those beliefs*—and thus to create all of its own miseries.

Finally, the human race believes that it is not possible to disavow its basic beliefs, or to recreate them, because it does not, and cannot, know how. The human race believes in ignorance.

These are the Ten Illusions of Humans, and they are a very big part of earthly reality. Still, you can change this.

SO HOW DO WE DO IT?

The first thing you must do is really understand the problem, which you are doing here, and then look at solutions. The solutions are to change your most basic beliefs and to assist others in changing theirs.

OKAY. BUT I WANT TO MAKE SURE BEFORE I HEAR ABOUT SOLUTIONS THAT WE DO HAVE THE POWER TO PRODUCE THEM. I DON'T WANT TO BE LED

DOWN THE GARDEN PATH HERE. I MEAN, WE *CAN* DO THIS, RIGHT? EVEN THOUGH NO ONE'S DONE IT BEFORE?

No one's had it explained to them before with this kind of clarity.

More and more people are seeing clearly now that the problems confronting the human race are real—and could destroy their species and its home—and more and more people are hearing with greater clarity how they can help in doing something about it.

That's what makes this a very important time. That's why *this book* "fell" into your hands when it did.

Yes, you have the power to recreate your reality on Earth in a new way. Absolutely. That's where your power to create—your Original Power—comes in. But that may be the first belief you have to change. You may have to change the belief that you do not have this power.

BECAUSE—AND NOW WE'RE BACK TO WHERE WE WERE BEFORE—WHAT WE BELIEVE, WE EXPERIENCE.

Exactly. And some things are harder to believe than others, so those things are harder to experience.

327

LIKE WHAT?

Well, it's easier to imagine that you're going to find a parking space right where you want it than it is to imagine that disunity or separation does not exist, or that condemnation does not exist, or that ignorance does not exist. So, many people are willing to try to produce what you would call "smaller results" by using Original Power, but they do not use that power to create what you would call larger results, because they do not believe they can.

In the same way, some people can experience small, negative life encounters as gifts (they call them "blessings in disguise"), while they experience other, larger, negative life encounters as struggles and dramas (they call them "misfortunes" or "tragedies"). They believe they can transform the smaller ones, but they don't believe they can transform the larger.

Masters are people who believe that they can use Original Power (or what some people call the power of God, or the power of prayer) to create *anything*—and so, they produce what you would term "miracles."

SO IF I BELIEVE THAT MY LIFE DOESN'T HAVE TO BE THE WAY IT IS, AND THAT THE WHOLE WORLD,

FOR THAT MATTER, CAN BE CHANGED, THEN IT CAN BE.

Yes. That is how the changes that *have* been made have come about. Somebody, some-where, believed that it could happen. And it did. Usually because that particular person helped *make* it happen.

That's why I said earlier, do not give up hope, do not ever stop trying to change your life or change the world.

All of you have come here, to this book, to this moment, to begin the next part of your journey. It is a journey to hopefulness. A journey to wholeness. It is the journey home.

This is about waking up, getting what's going on. This is about living your life in a new way, with intention and purpose and clarity and more fun than you ever thought possible.

Remember the Three-Way Path?

Have fun.

Spread joy.

Share love.

Man, are you going to have a chance to do *that* in the years ahead!

Are you ready?

Good! Start now.

Start now.

Today at home. Tomorrow at school.

Start now.

This is all it will take. That's why it can be said with such certainty that none of this is too big for you. None of this is too much. Fun, joy, and love is *who you are*. It is *the natural you*. Just give in to that.

Have fun doing whatever you're doing. Yes, even going to school. Just have *fun* with it. See it for what it is—a stepping-stone on the path to the greatest life you could ever hope to live.

Have fun with everything. It is possible. Just take the drama out of it, take the stress out of it. It's all good.

Spread joy around you. You can do that with something as simple as a smile, a laugh, a word of encouragement to a fellow traveler, a favor for a friend, a helping hand for a parent.

Share love with everyone, in the form that your soul tells you is most appropriate to the moment and to the kind of relationship that you have with each person—and with yourself.

Go now and create your world as you would have it be. Go now and celebrate your life, and everything that makes you "you."

Go now and re-create yourself *anew* in the next grandest version of the greatest vision you ever had about who you are.

This is my invitation. This is your dream. This is our next grand adventure.

A Closing Word . . .

I said at the beginning of this book that you have caused it to come into your hands, and so you have. You did so to empower yourself to hear, perhaps more clearly than ever before, truths that you have known forever in your heart, and that can change the world.

The events that occurred in the United States on September 11, 2001, have made it desperately obvious that our world *must* be changed, or soon there may be no world to change at all. Yet despite the horrible events of that terrible day, I come here to tell you in this closing message that this *can* be a more loving, peaceful world. Yours *can* be a more joyful experience. Ours *can* be a more fruitful life.

Millions of people around the globe, shocked at what happened on that September day, are now more motivated than ever to alter the way we live our lives on this planet. Yet, how can that be done? I believe I know of at least one very good way. Look to see, now, what it is you wish to experience—in your own life, and in the world—and then see if there is any way for you to be the *source* of that.

A central teaching of *Conversations with God* is: *What you wish to experience, provide for another.* So, if you wish to experience greater peace, love, and understanding, seek to provide greater peace, love, and understanding to all those whose lives you touch. If you wish to know that you are safe, cause another to know that he or she is safe. If you wish to better understand seemingly incomprehensible things, help others to better understand. If you wish to heal your own sadness or anger, seek to heal the sadness or anger of another.

In chapter 15 of this book I remember a young person asking, "Why do I always have to be the one to start?" I am reminded here of the wonderful soul-searching inquiry of the Jewish tradition: *If not now, when? If not me, who?*

It is you, it is our young people, who can bring us the change that can lead us away from the kind of insanities displayed on September 11, 2001. You can set the course for tomorrow, today.

There is much we can all do, but there is one

thing we cannot do. We cannot continue to cocreate our lives together on this planet as we have in the past. You already know this. Most young people do. You've been telling the world this for years, in everything from protests to poems to songs. Some of you are angry because you have not been heard. And right now, at this critical turning point in humanity's history, anger may not be inappropriate. It may, in fact, be a blessing. If you use your anger to pinpoint, not where the *blame* falls, but where the *cause* lies, you can lead the way to healing.

To me the cause seems obvious. It is discussed throughout this book. We are living in a world that operates on deep misunderstandings about life and how it is. Most humans have not learned the most basic lessons. Most humans have not remembered the most basic truths. Most have not understood the most basic spiritual wisdom. In short, most humans have not been listening to God, and because they have not, they watch themselves do ungodly things.

The message of *Conversations with God* is simple: We are all one. This is the message that the human race has largely ignored. Our separation mentality has underscored all of our human creations, and because our religions, our political structures, our economic systems, our educational institutions, and our whole approach to life have been based on the idea that we are separate from each other, we have inflicted all manner of injury upon each other. This injury has caused other injury, for like begets like, and negativity only breeds negativity.

Now the problem has reached planet-threatening proportions—and we should make no mistake about that. The human race has the power to annihilate itself. We can end life as we know it on this planet in one afternoon.

This is the first time in human history that we are able to say this. Before, we could destroy a village, or a city, or even a nation, but never the entire world in one day. Now, we can. And so I am asking all young people everywhere to focus your attention on the questions that such power places before you.

I hope that you will answer them from a spiritual perspective, not a political perspective, and not an economic perspective, from which they have been answered in the past.

I hope that you will have your own conversation with God, for only the grandest wisdom and the grandest truth can address the greatest problems, and we are now facing the greatest problems and the greatest challenges in the history of our species.

If you want what beauty there is in this world— and there is *so much* of it—to be experienced by your children and your children's children, I believe that you will have to become spiritual activists right here, right now. *You must choose to be at cause in the matter.*

That is the challenge that is placed before every thinking person today, young and old alike. But it is the young people who have the verve and the vigor, and the energy and the *real motivation* to meet this challenge. For the world of tomorrow will be the world that *you* experience—and the world that you will create.

I am asking you: Please, please, don't re-create the world as you see it today.

Please, be no more cynical about life, if ever you were. Please, be no longer disinterested in life, if ever you were. Please, let not one more day pass without your active involvement, right now, right where you are, in your homes, in your schools, in your communities, and in your world, in the movement to bring greater unity, understanding, harmony, and love to the human experience.

Become activists in helping others to change, at last, the age-old beliefs that have created the cruel, selfish, unkind, and inhuman behaviors you see all around you. Become one of The Changers, no longer content with simply talking about what's *not* working, but choosing now to join in creating what *will work*.

ReCreation, our nonprofit foundation, is forming an international alliance of young people making this choice. If you wish to connect with others around the globe who are joining together in activities and programs that could be world-altering, or are interested in bringing a local chapter to your community, please contact us today at:

> The Changers
> c/o The ReCreation Foundation
> PMB #1150 — 1257 Siskiyou Blvd.
> Ashland, OR 97520
> Telephone: 541-201-0019

> On the World Wide Web at **thechangers.org**
> e-mail address: thechangers@cwg.cc

Now let me say good-bye to you, my young friends. I hope the conversation here has served you well, and will bring you to a greater willingness to live from your inner wisdom and your inner truth every day of your life. The world of tomorrow is yours. Create it as the best world there ever was. I send you love.

> *Neale Donald Walsch*
> *Ashland, Oregon*
> *September 12, 2001*

Endnotes

1. This is an example of an "endnote." It is referenced in the first paragraph of chapter 4 of this book.

2. Also, ask them to read *How to Talk So Kids Will Listen & Listen So Kids Will Talk* by Adele Faber and Elaine Mazlish, the most effective book on parental communication that I have ever come across.

3. There are places in virtually every city where you can find emotional support during this time. One such place is an organization called P-Flag—Parents and Friends of Lesbians and Gays—which can be easily found on the Internet (www.pflag.com) and which often lists local chapters in the telephone book.

Here are some additional resources, all of them reachable without having to have access to a computer:

The Trevor Project: 1-800-850-8078. This nonprofit organization named for the short film about a 13-year-old boy who attempts suicide because of his sexuality has established a national toll-free, 24-hour suicide prevention hotline for gay youths.

The Gay and Lesbian National Hotline: 1-888-THE-GLNH (1-888-843-4564) Monday–Friday 4 P.M.–midnight, Saturday noon–5 P.M. EST. PMB #296, 2261 Market Street, San Francisco, CA 94114. Administrative phone: 1-888-415-3022, fax: 415-552-5498, www.glnh.org; e-mail: glnh@glnh.org

Hetrick-Martin Institute, 2 Astor Place, New York, NY 10003, 212-674-2400. The program of this institute is for youth from 12 to 21 years of age. The Institute believes all young people, regardless of sexual orientation or identity, deserve a safe and supportive environment in which to achieve their full potential. HMI creates this environment for lesbian, gay, and questioning youth between the ages of 12 and 21 and their families. Through a comprehensive package of direct services and referrals, HMI seeks to foster healthy youth development. HMI's staff promotes excellence in the delivery of youth services and uses its expertise to create innovative programs that other organizations may use as models.

National Suicide Hotline 1-800-SUICIDE

SAVE—Suicide Awareness Voices of Education, 952-946-7998, Minneapolis, MN 55424-0507, www.save.org; e-mail address: save@winternet.com—an organization dedicated to educating the public about suicide prevention.

Covenant House (800-999-9999) receives annually over 84,000 crisis calls from youngsters all over the United States who need immediate help and have nowhere else to turn. Covenant House is the largest privately funded childcare agency in the United States, providing shelter and service to homeless and runaway youth. It was incorporated in New York City in 1972 and has since expanded in the United States to Anchorage, Atlantic City, Detroit, Fort Lauderdale, Houston, Los Angeles, Newark, New Orleans, Oakland, Orlando, Philadelphia, St. Louis, Washington, D.C., and, outside the United States, to Toronto, Vancouver, Guatemala, Honduras, Mexico, and Nicaragua. In addition to food, shelter, clothing, and crisis care, Covenant House provides a variety of services to homeless youth including health care, education, vocational preparation, drug abuse treatment and prevention programs, legal services, recreation, mother/child programs, transitional living programs, street outreach, and aftercare. www.covenanthouse.org

4. Accurate information on HIV/AIDS is available from AIDS and Young People, an Internet site that explains what the disease is, what causes it, and how people become infected. Includes tips for safer sex. Found at www.avert. org. Other resources include *AIDS Handbook: An Intro-*

duction, information about the HIV virus and its transmission; about AIDS and its treatment. Written and illustrated by Eastchester Middle School students for other students, and found at www.westnet.com/~rickd/AIDS/AIDS1.html. *AIDS: Education and Prevention from the Growing Epidemic,* tells what the disease is, how it is transmitted, how many people have died as a result of it, and what young people can do to protect themselves from it, found at library.thinkquest.org/10631. *Can I Get AIDS?* tells how AIDS is spread and how to protect yourself against it, found at kidshealth.org.

5. *Spirit Matters* is a brilliant book that dynamically describes things we can do, right here, right now, to allow society to jointly create the "point of life" so that it can be what most young people would like it to be. The author of *Spirit Matters,* Michael Lerner, says we should create a radically different "bottom line" in our world, a new set of corporate and personal values that redefine success and what it means to be human. His book offers some of the most important and exciting statements ever made on this subject. It is jammed with innovative and daring ideas, and I would love to see a ton of you guys read it—especially those of you who are now considering careers and the jobs you will do as you move into your twenties and step out into the larger world. You can make changes in that world—I'm telling you, you *really* can—if you are willing to be one of The Changers. This book gives you a whole pile of fascinating and "politically incorrect" ideas on some of the ways that might be accomplished.

6. If the portion of the conversation dealing with personal "faults" struck a chord, you will really want to read a book called *The Dark Side of the Light Chasers,* by Debbie Ford. It's about loving the "shadow side" of ourselves—the part of our human nature that we have always condemned and "made wrong." Or that others have made wrong. This is really a fabulous book for teenagers to get hold of. Go get it. You'll love it.

7. Check out www.freevibe.com—a teen-oriented site providing information about drugs and their danger.

8. Persons interested in starting such a school may wish to contact The Heartlight Learning Community, a worldwide alternative education movement based on the teachings in *Conversations with God,* at Heartlight Education, PMB #91, 1257 Siskiyou Blvd., Ashland, OR 97520; telephone: 541-482-1120; on the Internet at www.HeartlightEducation.org; e-mail address: heartlighteducation@cwg.cc.

9. *The Power of Positive Thinking* is a very special book that everyone would benefit from reading. It was written by Dr. Norman Vincent Peale, a minister, in the middle of the last century. I believe that you can draw enormous value from this incredible little book—even though it was written more than 50 years ago—regardless of whether Dr. Peale's religious point of view is one you share. It is available through most libraries and can be purchased on the Internet.

10. *Excuse Me, Your LIFE Is Waiting* is an incredible and very breezy, enjoyable, easy-to-read book by Lynn Grabhorn that talks about this exact subject and gives you tools with which to change your thinking and change your life. You will love it.

11. www.yesworld.org—YES—Youth for Environmental Sanity—is a nonprofit organization that educates, inspires, and empowers young people to join forces for social justice and environmental sanity. Youth stand at a threshold point in life, as they make choices that will send out vast ripples. Some young people believe growing up means abandoning their ideals. To this organization it means learning how to live the highest ideals every day, on the Earth. YES believes that if the passion, creativity, and commitment of youth can be liberated for the common good, they can transform our world.

About the Author

NEALE DONALD WALSCH lives with his wife, Nancy, at a retreat they have founded in the woodlands of southern Oregon. Together they have formed ReCreation, an organization whose goal is to give people back to themselves. Walsch is continually touring the country, answering requests for lectures, and hosting workshops to support and spread the messages contained in the *Conversations with God* books.

Conversations with God
for teens

also available in hardcover
from Hampton Roads
ISBN 1-57174-263-8
$19.95